NORTH STAR BOOKS

The Greatest
Cattle Drive

PAUL I. WELLMAN

Illustrated by Lorence Bjorklund

HOUGHTON MIFFLIN COMPANY BOSTON

The Riverside Press Cambridge

To the two youngest WELLMANS
SCOTT and PAUL
with a pat of grandfatherly
approval on the back of each
of them.

Paul I. Wellman has proved in many books that he knows, loves and respects the West. In previous NORTH STARS he has passed along to young Americans his profound understanding of the vast region westward of the Mississippi where less than a century ago buffalo grazed by the millions, proud and fierce Indian tribes disputed the westward expansion of frontiersmen, and fortunes were still to be made in gold, silver and pioneer railroad building.

In THE GREATEST CATTLE DRIVE this western historian takes up the dramatic role played by cattle and cattlemen who eventually supplanted the buffalo and the Indians. This true account of an almost incredible cattle drive, achieved by Nelson Story and his men in 1866, reads like the most exciting fiction but is based soundly upon facts wherever facts are available. Story was the first to realize that the Montana gold camps were rich in precious metal, but actually in danger of starvation, while Texas was overrun with longhorn cattle but sorely in need of money.

How Nelson Story, starting from Texas with a herd of 1000 cattle and a crew of 24 men, braved stampedes, flooded rivers, enraged Indian tribes, waterless deserts and mountain blizzards to bring the cattle over unmapped trails to the Montana gold camps is an experience no young reader will ever forget. This is Wellman at his vivid and informative best.

STERLING NORTH
General Editor

Books By PAUL I. WELLMAN

Novels
BRONCHO APACHE
JUBAL TROOP
ANGEL WITH SPURS
THE BOWL OF BRASS
THE WALLS OF JERICHO
THE CHAIN
THE IRON MISTRESS
THE COMANCHEROS
THE FEMALE
JERICHO'S DAUGHTERS
RIDE THE RED EARTH
THE FIERY FLOWER
MAGNIFICENT DESTINY

Histories
DEATH ON THE PRAIRIE
DEATH IN THE DESERT
   (REPUBLISHED TOGETHER AS
      THE INDIAN WARS OF THE WEST)
THE TRAMPLING HERD
GLORY, GOD AND GOLD
A DYNASTY OF WESTERN OUTLAWS
SPAWN OF EVIL

Reminiscence
PORTAGE BAY

Biography
STUART SYMINGTON

For Younger Readers
GOLD IN CALIFORNIA
INDIAN WARS AND WARRIORS (EAST)
INDIAN WARS AND WARRIORS (WEST)
RACE TO THE GOLDEN SPIKE
THE GREATEST CATTLE DRIVE

CONTENTS

Note To The Reader

Nelson Story was too much a man of action to leave any detailed written record of his doings. His own personal account of his great cattle drive across half a continent occupies at most a few paragraphs.

By using various types of other information, however, the chronicler is able to reconstruct events which Story dismissed with perhaps a sentence, like "We swam the herd across the river," or "The cattle stampeded and we rounded them up" — giving little notion of the difficulties and dangers encountered.

The historical records of the time, geographical features known, events similar to those he experienced told in detail by others, and especially statements of men who were with Story, or who saw him and commented on various occasions, have been relied on to present as full an account as possible. Wherever specific evidence is available it is presented faithfully.

By such means the author hopes not only to have drawn a picture of the kind of man Nelson Story was, but also to give the modern reader some knowledge of the action, color, and perils of cattle drives in general, and why they took place, and how.

PAUL I. WELLMAN

THAT SPRING DAY the cattle hunters had decided to comb a very large thicket, where they believed many wild cattle were hiding.

Stated in such a way, the task sounds simple. Actually it would be about as dangerous, difficult, and painful as can well be imagined.

In the first place there was the thicket itself, a great area of thorny trees and dagger-spiked lesser growth — mesquite, blackjack, chaparral, cactus, and many others — all twisted together in a mass so thick it seemed almost solid. The men must ride through it, not at a walk, but frequently at a breakneck gallop.

Then there were the cattle. "Outlaws" they were called, wild as deer, able to run almost as fast, and sometimes dangerous when their uncertain tempers were aroused.

The cattle hunters themselves, some white, some Mexican, one who was half Indian, half Negro, were picturesque, though little resembling cowboys of the open range. No big hats were seen here, or any fancy trappings to be caught by branches. Close-fitting leather chaps, brush-jackets of canvas or leather, boots, *tapederos* (toe-fenders) on the stirrups, leather gloves — these men were practically armored. Yet even such protection was not enough to guard them entirely. Not one in the crowd of a dozen or more but had scars on his face — and others on his body or legs — to show how the thorn country dealt with those who invaded it.

Ramon, a little Mexican, with a wise, seamed face, was *caporal* — the boss of this group. With a few words he sent his men to form a wide arc, reserving for himself the place of greatest responsibility, the outside post. They knew which way to go. Weeks ago a corral had been built in the thicket, with wide wings to guide cattle into the entrance. Today there was also, not far from that corral, a "decoy herd" of tame cattle — "tame," that is, according to Texas standards — which would play a part in the drive.

This was southern Texas, the year was 1866, and there was no easy way to catch outlaw cattle as every man knew.

Ramon, looking almost like a monkey, perched on his horse, was an expert cattle hunter and a superb rider. He waited until his companions had time to take their stations, and then guided his horse straight toward that forbidding tangle of thorny growth.

Now it could be seen that here and there were trails — really tunnels through the tangled brush. These, Ramon knew, were made by outlaw cattle, which liked to keep in the dark jungles during the day, and go out at night to graze in more open spaces.

He took one of these trails, bending low over his saddle horn to avoid tangling branches overhead. It

was crooked, as he expected, and he could see only a little way ahead. Thorns, stubs, and limbs of trees were laced together about and above him. But down that trail he must go.

The horse knew his business. He was a small Spanish gelding, alert and quick, fast for a short distance, and like his rider willing to take punishment, game to the last, and so wise that he hardly needed reining.

All at once, up ahead, there was a snort and a crash. It was followed by others. Wild cattle had heard or smelled the rider and were heading away from him.

Ramon continued along the trail, watching out for treacherous branches. He felt that he was in luck, for he had flushed quite a little band of outlaws. Now he must keep them going toward the corral, and toward the decoy herd waiting.

This easy pace could not last long. Suddenly there were more crashes — this time to the right, which meant to the *outside* of the surround.

Man and horse knew their duty. Without hesitation the little Mexican swung his mount over in that direction, for it was a point of honor to turn all cattle in.

Now the brush rider showed the stuff of which he and the others of his kind were made. No time to hunt an open way — even if one existed — so Ramon and his horse must crash right *through* the tangle of thorny growth.

Away they went, hurtling into the fierce jungle. Now Ramon rode "all over his horse," as the saying was. Sometimes he was stretched low over his neck, sometimes alongside him, then over on the other side, almost under him at times, and all the while he must keep his eyes open, watching for hooking stubs and thorny branches or have his eyes gouged out. To shield himself he used his hands, arms, and shoulders, but even so a stub raked him across the forehead, opening a bleeding cut.

The horse, too, suffered, his chest and legs bruised and bleeding from thorns. But it never occurred to either the mount or the man to hesitate. On they drove, "tearing a hole through the brush," which immediately closed behind them. Suddenly, just ahead they saw three or four steers. These outlaws, wide-horned and wild, looked at them with starting eyes, then turned and galloped in the desired direction.

Over and over, this was repeated. Ramon's men were getting punishment, too, but perhaps not as much as he. Nevertheless, he willingly accepted an extra share, for he was the leader.

All at once, just ahead in a narrow lane, the little

Mexican saw an outlaw that did not run. A bull, this
time, mean-tempered and powerful. He was black,
fierce, with huge, keen, forward-pointing horns. At
the sight of the man on the horse, he braced himself
and lowered his huge head.

M. Bozeman, the pioneer who laid out the Bozeman Trail; John X. Beidler, who ran a freight wagon service and never shot except to kill; Captain Jim Williams, who never backed away from a fight in his life; Colonel W. F. Sanders, who became head of the Vigilantes and later a United States senator; and others, less honorable, like the killer Joseph A. Slade, the deadly smooth Henry Plummer, and members of his murder gang like the ferocious George Ives and Boone Helm.

And there also was Nelson Story.

The West used to say of a man with unusual courage that he had "gravel in his gizzard." Nobody had more gravel in his gizzard than Nelson Story. At this time, in 1863, he was twenty-five years old, quiet-spoken and polite, but with a look in his eye that warned men to take no liberties with him. He had taken a mining claim in Alder Gulch, but at first he did not have much time to work it — he was too busy doing other things.

Story was born in Burlingham, Ohio. He had some schooling — enough to teach in a country school one winter — but when he went out to the West in 1856, he was only eighteen years old, a slim, lanky youth, who reached Fort Leavenworth, on the Missouri River, with just thirty-six dollars in his pocket.

He had to find work, so he began by cutting posts

and splitting fence rails, which he sold. After a time he acquired a few work oxen, and hired out to plow land for owners. Gradually he got some condemned government wagons, which he loaded with dry goods and groceries, and began freighting them to Denver, Colorado.

This was hard, sometimes dangerous work. Though freighters usually went in companies of several wagons, the Cheyenne Indians were bad at the time, and there was often some fighting to do. Once Story lost all his freighter stock in an Indian raid, except for a blind mule and a lame ox. With these he managed to reach Leavenworth with one empty wagon.

Such setbacks would have discouraged some young men, but not Nelson Story. He had more than his share of determination; but he had more — someone who inspired him.

In Leavenworth he had met a pretty, charming girl named Ellen Trent. She was slim and graceful as a young birch tree, and she had more than her share of spunk. No wonder she began to take up a large part of young Nelson Story's thinking. But he had suffered a severe loss from the Indian raid, and he had to make a stake before he could even think of getting married.

So he went back to Colorado, where the gold mines were booming. There must have been an understanding of some kind between them before he left Leavenworth for the mountains.

He was not afraid of work, and he had some skill at carpentry. In later years he said he built flumes in the Colorado mining areas, and because wages were high — since most men preferred digging for gold, or hunting for it, to any other kind of labor — he laid enough money by so that early in 1862 he felt able to return to Fort Leavenworth and Ellen Trent.

They were married, and Ellen accompanied her new husband to the mountain country, and shared with him the dangers and hardships that followed.

Those dangers and hardships were very real. Shortly after the courageous young pioneer couple arrived in Denver, news came of a new excitement to the north. Gold was found in July, 1862, at Grasshopper Creek in what is now Montana, and a town named Bannack sprang up. Nelson Story was building up his freighting business again, and the following spring, of 1863, he and Ellen decided to go to the new mining area where things were booming.

He had two wagons now, with ox teams, but because

he knew how difficult it would be to get goods into the rough mountains, he also bought a string of eleven pack mules.

These, and the wagons, he loaded with goods of various kinds, including flour, sugar, bacon, molasses, and various household articles besides some bolts of cloth. He hired a couple of men to help with the outfit, and he and Ellen set out for Montana.

They arrived at Bannack on June 4, 1863. To their astonishment the town was practically deserted. Only nine days before, on May 26, as previously recounted, the Alder Gulch strike had been made. Most of Bannack's population was gone in the rush to the new diggings some fifty miles east.

It took Nelson Story no time at all to make up his mind. All those people (about 10,000 arrived at Alder Gulch in the first month) would need food. He left his wagons and work oxen at Bannack, found a boarding place for his wife, and with his eleven pack mules and his riding horse, headed for the new excitement.

At Virginia City his goods were bought as soon as he arrived, and there was great demand for the transportation his pack animals could give. He did take time to stake out a claim, but he did not at once work

it, and it would be many months before he even knew
if it contained any gold.

Meantime he went back to Bannack, and brought
his bride over the rough mountain trail to Alder Gulch.
They established a little store in a log cabin he built
at Summit (next to Virginia City), and Ellen, a smiling,
busy little person, helped by baking and selling pies
and cakes to the hungry miners.

But now Nelson Story found himself for a period
forgetting about his business or his mining, because
he had to face a peril that for a time terrified even the
rough miners.

In the midst of all the brawling industry of the mining country, a secret gang of murderers and robbers was operating. Its chief was a smooth, evil killer, named Henry Plummer, a man of mystery whose origins were never known, although it was learned much later than this time that he shot at least two men to death before he was forced to flee first California, then Nevada, for the Montana country.

Plummer was somewhat above middle height, lithe, active, and graceful, with a neat brown mustache and deceptively pleasant features. Very careful of his appearance and clothes, he passed as a gentleman — so much so that he got himself elected sheriff at Bannack.

But Plummer had no interest in upholding the law. He wanted the title and office of sheriff merely to use as a mask for carrying on criminal activities which were his real interest and for which he had planned. Very soon he gathered about him a gang of outlaws, many of whom were killers of long standing. Even his deputy sheriffs were highway robbers — "road agents" as the West called them. At least fifty men became members of his secret organization, ranging from spies who informed when gold shipments were moving and reported enemies of the gang who should be

"eliminated," to cruel and wanton killers who sometimes slew for the mere thrill of it.

The criminals adopted the title of "Innocents," had
passwords, corresponded in cipher, and kept watchers
at every stage station to mark men for robbery, often
for murder. Nobody knew who they were, but their
depredations soon were apparent to everyone.

In her very first days at Virginia City, Ellen Story
was the horrified witness of a murder when a man
named Dillingham was shot down before her eyes.
The victim, it later developed, was a road agent who
was killed by three members of his own gang because
they suspected that he might inform against them.

The murder Ellen Story saw was one of the first
committed by the Plummer gang, but the killings soon
grew in numbers. Shortly, a wave of terror gripped
the mountain country. Stages, freight wagons, men
on horseback, pedestrians, were held up, robbed, and
all too frequently shot down by road agents. At least
one hundred and two persons were murdered during
the reign of Plummer's gang.

But there were courageous men in Virginia City,
who dared to fight this terror of lawlessness, of which
the evil "Sheriff," Henry Plummer, was the secret chief

and director. In those early days, when the enforce-
ment of all laws broke down, it sometimes became
necessary for the good citizens to take matters into
their own hands. A committee of such men in Virginia
City formed to fight the road agents, and took the
name of Vigilantes, which had been used in other
places by similar groups under the same circumstances.

Late in December of 1863, a young German named
Nicholas Thibalt was found brutally murdered. The
Vigilantes investigated the case, and arrested a man
named George Ives, Plummer's chief lieutenant, when
they got sure evidence that he was the slayer.

Ives was tried in the little mining camp of Nevada
City, a suburb of Virginia City, before a miners' jury
of twenty-four men. Colonel Sanders acted as prose-
cutor, and Robert Hereford was the acting sheriff.
Twenty-three of the twenty-four jurors voted the
prisoner guilty and sentenced him to hang.

At that the crowd of about fifteen hundred men who
had witnessed the trial, which was held in the open air
in the street, decided to hang Ives at once.

But a hitch occurred — and the Virginia City district
for the first time had a sample of the courage of Nelson
Story.

On the roofs of buildings overlooking the scene of the trial, figures of men appeared. They were members of Plummer's gang, outlaws who were ready to rescue Ives.

At the news, a near panic ran through the crowd. Men grew fainthearted, and even Hereford, the acting sheriff, hid around the corner of a building for protection.

Story was not at that time a Vigilante, but he believed Ives was guilty, and he believed something must be done to halt the reign of terror. Seeing the hesitation and fear of the people in the street, he knew that somebody must take the risk of facing those gunmen on the rooftops.

He was armed with two six-shooters and a carbine, and beside him stood a man named Benjamin Ezekiel, keeper of a boardinghouse.

"Come on, Ben," he said.

The two of them, weapons leveled, stepped forward, their eyes on those threatening gunmen above.

"Go ahead and carry out justice," said Story to the miners' court.

"Some of the crowd," he related long after, "threw themselves on the ground, actually falling over each other," for they feared that shooting would begin and did not wish to be in the line of fire.

But young Story's resolute stand quelled the outlaws. Ives was hanged, and the first blow was struck at the Plummer gang.

Immediately after this, Story was invited to join the Vigilantes, and accepted. These men were sworn to put an end to crime in the mountain country. They knew that to be enemies of the road agents meant possible death for themselves any day, and at the same time they hardly knew whom they could trust. They did not even know exactly who their foes were. Yet they met together and set out to restore order and peace. The names of those men are still preserved, and Nelson Story is listed on the roster of the Vigilantes of Virginia City, which became famous in the history of the West.

They were outnumbered, but they went to work at once to do what they were sworn to do. This is not to be a recital of the campaign that winter against the outlaws. What has been told is only to show the bravery and leadership of Nelson Story. It is enough to say that as they collected evidence the Vigilantes struck swiftly, fiercely. All together twenty-four proven members of the outlaw gang were killed in gun battles or executed by hanging. These included Plummer himself, who died on the gallows with two of his men, January 10, 1864. By the end of September, 1865, every one of the Plummer gang was dead or had fled from the country never to return.

The work of the Vigilantes was finished. Law and safety returned to the mountains and it was time for new and honest legal officers to take over. Nelson Story went back to his personal affairs, transporting goods with his string of pack mules, and operating his little log cabin store where his brave young wife Ellen had continued to wait on customers and keep their home bright and cheerful through all this perilous crisis.

He had not yet even tried to work his claim in the gulch, even though claims on each side of it were producing gold richly. But early in 1866, he was warned that a man named Bill Carter was going to "jump" his claim, in other words, to take possession of it unlawfully.

Nelson Story never looked for trouble, but if trouble came he never backed away from it. Before dawn next morning, he was on his claim, ready to defend it.

Sure enough, as daylight came, Carter appeared

with some other men to take over the place. The new-comers were startled to hear Story's voice: "Stand off!"

But Carter was determined. Seizing one of the men with him and using his body as a shield, he drew his six-shooter to kill Story, knowing the young man would hesitate to shoot down an unarmed opponent such as the one who was unwillingly acting as a protection for Carter.

What the claim jumper did not count on was the kind of shooting Story could do. The young man waited until he saw Carter's pistol hand come over the shoulder of the man in front. Then he fired — shattering the hand and hurling the gun out of it to the ground.

This kind of "shooting" has often been portrayed in moving pictures and television shows, where blank cartridges and camera tricks are used. It looks easy, but actually it was the most difficult of shots, almost impossible to make without hitting the man who was acting as a shield. Not more than one or two instances of similar shots can be found in all the real Western history.

Carter groped for his pistol with his crippled hand. He could not pick it up, and he and his gang fled from the scene.

The incident caused Nelson Story to decide to work his claim. He did so, and was more than lucky, for he struck a placer that yielded him gold dust and nuggets worth $30,000.*

Story now faced the problem of what to do with his money. He was an unusual young man, in many respects, one of which was that he could think a long way ahead. Having studied the California gold rush, he was struck by the fact that the men who gained the largest fortunes were not the gold miners, but the suppliers of food, tools, and other necessities to those miners.

He also saw — what nobody else seemed to see — that unless somebody did something about it there might be starvation in those mountains. He resolved that even if he had to risk his life and all he had, he would forestall that hunger time.

* Nelson Story was a kindly man. In later years when his former enemy, Bill Carter, was "down and out," Story supported him financially for the rest of his life.

NELSON STORY had heard that there were many cattle in Texas, and it was at this time that he had his inspiration to turn Montana gold, which Texas needed, into cattle, which Montana needed.

To do so he must go to that remote and, to him, strange place, Texas, buy a herd, and bring it back overland to Montana. This was to be a task more difficult than he perhaps then imagined. But he undertook it with his typical pluck.

He had to leave Mrs. Story in Virginia City, but Ellen had plenty of courage also. They found a friendly couple with whom she could board, since it was impossible for her to make the kind of journey her husband was planning, and she kissed him goodbye and told him not to worry about her but to come back as soon as he could.

Then, carrying his gold in a heavy tin box which he had especially made (and which is still a treasured relic in the Story family of today), he went south by stagecoach to Salt Lake City. This was not the route he intended to take on his return journey with his cattle, but Salt Lake City was the nearest place where he could conduct his business quickly.

From Salt Lake City he expressed his gold to a banking firm, Kountze Brothers, of New York City. Then he followed his gold to the East, part way by stage, and the rest by railroad.

In New York, Kountze Brothers offered to pay him $40,000 in greenbacks for his $30,000 worth of gold. This was because paper money had gone down in value during the recently concluded Civil War. Nelson Story had faith in his nation, and he gladly took paper currency, at the added figure. His faith was soon justified. It did not take the nation long to bring the greenbacks to full value again, so this proved a very good investment.

A letter of credit from Kountze Brothers was all he needed, when he returned to Fort Leavenworth, Kansas. Most business at that time was done through letters of credit or drafts on banks. But Nelson Story took $10,000 in greenbacks and sewed the money in

his clothes, to hide it from robbers. He knew that cash would bring him better cattle at better prices than if he tried to buy on delivery to some distant place.

At Fort Leavenworth he also found two young men, Bill Petty and Tom Allen, whom he had known before. They were friends he could trust, and he hired them to ride south with him. The three of them reached Fort Worth, Texas, in the early summer of 1866.

There were many cattle around Fort Worth. Word had come down from the north that there was some sort of trouble up there, and trail drivers hesitated about starting up the trail. Story had heard something of this difficulty, but he began buying cattle as if it were no problem at all.

Looking over all the herds within riding distance, he picked out a thousand animals, the best he could find. Many of them were "cows with calves at side," which meant they were not intended for the butcher, at least not immediately. Others were steers, and some were bulls. It was what was known as a "mixed herd," and some of the cattlemen looked at him in wonder when he said he intended driving his cattle north. In those first days of trail driving, beef cattle, for which cash might quickly be realized, were what men generally took to the faraway markets.

By the time he had his thousand cattle, and a horse herd to mount his riders, he had invested his $10,000. It was a lot of money for that day, and particularly for the risks involved, because he intended to take that herd through the most dangerous country in America.

When he left Montana the mining towns were almost in a state of siege. A red circle of Sioux, Cheyenne, Blackfoot, and Arapaho warriors had cut the isolated gold camps off from the rest of the world. Men who tried to pass through that cordon often died, and if their bodies were found at all they were usually scalped and mangled by the savages.

Yet Nelson Story intended to break through that barrier of hostile tribes, and he needed men upon whom he could depend in a tight place — tough men, brave men.

To find those men he watched the wide-hatted, tan-faced cowboys he saw in the streets of Fort Worth, or in the saloons and gambling places. With some of them he talked. He, himself, was originally an Ohio man, and his sympathies in the Civil War were with the North. But these cowboys almost all were ex-Confederates.

That did not bother Nelson Story. The war was over. Besides, there was something about those reckless, unrepentant Rebels that he liked. Southern generals, such as Robert E. Lee and Stonewall Jackson, had liked them when they marched in the Southern armies. Northern generals, such as Ulysses S. Grant and William Tecumseh Sherman, had respected them when their Union armies fought against them. The Texas Brigade in Lee's gray hosts were called "the Grenadiers of the Confederacy," which meant they were about the finest fighting men in that remarkable fighting force.

These young men in Fort Worth were leather-tough and weather-beaten. Some of them perhaps drank a little too much — when they could get it. A few of them may even have had "Wanted" signs posted for them in other parts of the country, for men were quick on the trigger, and shootings were common in Texas over wrongs, real or fancied.

Story knew they would fight if there was fighting to do. And also that they could ride, knew horses and cattle, and made light of hardship, however severe it was.

So he began to hire men, picking them carefully. With him were his two riders from Fort Leavenworth, Bill Petty and Tom Allen. To fill his crew he chose twenty-two Texans. Most of them were daredevil

young cowboys, with, in many cases, war service behind them. One was the camp cook, who would drive
the chuck wagon and prepare the meals — older than
the others,· but a tough veteran plainsman, with a
bleached mustache, who took no nonsense from the
skylarking youngsters.

Counting himself, there were now twenty-five in the
crew. He knew that if these men were to do what
he wanted them to do, and go where he would take
them, he must win their respect and loyalty.

Nelson Story was twenty-eight years old, not much

older than some of his men, younger than the camp cook. But he called them together and spoke quietly:

"Boys, I'm going to take you on the wildest, longest, roughest, maybe riskiest trail any of you have ever seen. But I judge you are men, which is why I picked you. I'm the boss on this drive. If anyone doesn't like that, or doesn't want to go along, he can step out now, and no questions asked, and no hard feelings."

The men looked at him, and they liked what they saw. He had a level, straight look, and they could see

he was no blusterer; also that he would expect a certain amount of discipline from them. He seemed fair-minded, and was no part of a coward, and appeared to know what he was doing.

They perhaps thought to themselves that twenty-five riders were more men than a herd of a thousand cattle commonly needed. Usually a herd that size required no more than a dozen to sixteen men, including the camp cook and the trail boss. It was evident, therefore, that this was to be some sort of a special expedition.

So what? A tough trail? They were as tough as whang-leather themselves. Dangerous, perhaps? Not a man among them but had looked death between the eyes, many times, before this. Many of them had been soldiers, so they knew the value of a commander. Not a man dropped out.

Story's next move was to take them to the corrals where his horses were being held. It was customary to assign each cowboy his "string" of horses, usually six to each man. Four of the cow ponies would be good mounts — as cowboys considered good mounts — which meant they were speedy, quick at turning, knew how to behave when their riders roped an animal, and were practically tireless. It did *not* mean that they had to be gentle, or eat sugarplums out of a man's hand — they were more likely to bite the hand off! And nearly every one of them would do his best, first thing in the morning when he was saddled and mounted, to buck his rider out of his saddle.

In addition each man was assigned a couple of broncos — "bronks" to the cowboys — which were untrained to saddle or bridle. A cowboy was expected to break these wild horses during the course of a drive. That was freely accepted. A man who couldn't stay on a wickedly pitching bronco with steel-spring legs, sloping rump, and head down, ought not be in the cow business anyway. It was part of the fun (for those looking on, not for the rider). Nelson Story soon showed the boys that he could ride a mean horse with the best of them, and thus rose still higher in their confidence.

An unwritten law was that once a string of horses was turned over to a man they were the same as his own, as long as he was with the outfit. No one, not even the boss, rode one of a cowboy's ponies without his permission. Another thing: when a rider got his string, he received no information about his horses. He was expected to find out each animal's tricks himself, and for anyone to offer him suggestions was considered an offense, as showing lack of confidence in his riding ability. He was expected to know every horse in his string, whether he was a "cutting horse," a "circle horse," a "night horse," or just a plain, vicious, unbroken bronk which the cowboy must spend part of his time trying to convince that the man in the saddle was the boss, and eventually to be bridle-wise.

Altogether there were one hundred and fifty horses in the herd, and four mules for the chuck wagon. Those ponies not being ridden for the time being, must be brought along behind the herd by two men told off as "horse wranglers." Counting off the cook, the horse wranglers, and Story, who was the trail boss and must be everywhere, that left twenty-one riders for the herd.

Some days were spent branding the herd. Story's cattle carried a brand called the "Ox Yoke" on the left side and the "Circle" on the left hip. This branding was necessary so that animals could be identified in case others got mixed with them.

At last it was time to begin the great march north.

One morning, early in August, the young trail boss gave the order, "Start 'em moving!"

It is an always interesting sight to see a big herd string out. With shrill whoops the cowboys ride toward the mass of animals, urging them forward. For a time everything seems confused.

Some of the cattle, still wild as deer, try to break away, suspicious of this new movement. After each of these fugitives rides a cowboy at a hard gallop, leaning a little forward in his saddle with a whirling rope end in his hand, while his cow pony, with neck outstretched and hoofs in a rhythmic thunder, pursues the errant steer.

Away flees the steer, running at his best with surprising speed. But the pony, mane flying, eyes fairly gleaming with the joy of the chase, races as if this were a personal contest between him and the stubborn beast.

The horse gains, comes abreast of the running animal. The latter halts suddenly, gives a snort, and dodges off in a different direction.

From a dead run the pony comes to a stop in two jumps, doubles so quickly that as he leans over in his whirling turn his rider's stirrup literally brushes the earth, and is after the steer again. Another break or two like this, each time headed off by the pony which hardly needs to be guided, and the steer, with a final shake of his head, turns in the right direction and heads for the herd. Strangely, once there, in the midst of his fellows, the wildness leaves him, and he moves along with the others convoyed by the outriders.

While the runaways are being returned, there has been some "milling" in the center of the herd, because part of the cattle were headed in the wrong direction and have to straighten out. But presently all this confusion and disorder, creating perfect billows of dust, and accompanied by continual bellowing by the cattle, becomes a march, guided and led.

Up front two good cowpunchers, called "point riders," one on each side of the little group of leading

cattle, but well back of them, form what is called the "point." Behind the leaders the rest of the herd trails, gradually widening out toward the rear. From the cattle rises a continual noise — the clashing of horns, trampling of hoofs, bawling and bellowing — while the shrill yells of the herders add to the racket, all creating a wild medley of sound.

In the fog of dust, mounted figures appear dimly here and there on the outskirts of the herd on each side. These are the "swing men," and it is their duty to keep the herd reasonably compact and moving. Last of all, at the rear of the herd come the "drag riders." Theirs

is the most unpleasant duty — keeping the lazy, weak, or footsore cattle from falling too far behind the rest of the herd. When the weather is dry these men literally "eat the dust," which is kicked up by all those thousands of hoofs. Usually they ride with a bandanna handkerchief tied over their noses and mouths (leaving the eyes clear to see), for it aids them in breathing.

Meantime the veteran cook, called the *cocinero*, has hitched his four mules to the chuck wagon, and started off ahead. His sturdy vehicle contains not only food — "sowbelly" (salt pork), beans, flour, coffee, molasses, baking soda, and so on — together with the cooking utensils and tin plates for the men, but also the bedrolls of the crew. The cook also carries a shotgun as well as his six-shooter, and often he can vary the monotony of the diet he serves with prairie chicken, or venison, or even wild turkey. It is his duty to reach the agreed-on camping place and have supper ready when the herd arrives to be "bedded down," at which time the cowboys can take their turns at eating.

The horse wranglers bring along the *remuda* (extra mounts), sometimes at one side of the cattle herd, sometimes behind it. Those intelligent little horses soon grow to know they are somehow a part of the whole general march, and they stay with the cattle without much guidance.

As for the trail boss, his duties are many. First, he must set the direction and pace. He it is who rides far ahead to find water and grass where the herd can graze until it is ready to lie down at night. He must know how to handle men, make decisions, see that everything goes smoothly. Sometimes he may be miles out in front, looking for a good bedding ground. At other times he can be seen coasting up and down the outskirts of the herd, speaking to each cowboy as he passes, looking over the cattle, constantly in the saddle from long before dawn until far after dark.

So Nelson Story and his cattle outfit started for the north.

"For the first three or four days," he told his men at the beginning, "we've got to keep the cows* moving fast."

The men nodded, for they understood these instructions. Cattle are nervous about leaving a country with which they are familiar, and may try to turn back.

---

* Cattle in general were called cows, although individuals were known by terms more exact, as bulls, cows, steers, calves, and so on.

If this movement grows it can make a herd hard to manage.

So Story's ex-Confederate cowboys raised the long yell, "*Yip-yip-yip-yipeeeeee! Yah-ah-ah-yay-yeeeee-eeee!*" It was the shrill cattle yell, keyed to the wild mockery of the coyotes on the plains, and it had been carried back to the army of General Lee by the young Texans who went to Virginia to fight in gray uniforms. The other Confederate regiments promptly adopted the yell as their own, so that it became known in countless battles as the "Rebel Yell."

That yell — cowboy or rebel, depending on the time and circumstances — and the wild riders showing up out of the dust on every side with swinging lariat ends (bullwhips were not used in trailing cattle), kept the herd going along at such a pace that the cattle did not even think of trying to turn back. When they reached the bedding ground at night they were too tired to do anything but rest.

Of course this continued only for three or four days. After that the herd, accustomed to traveling, was allowed to take a slower pace, for it must graze a good part of the journey north to keep in good condition.

At night the resting longhorns were watched by relays of cowboys, who took regular two-hour shifts

at riding around the outskirts of the herd. They rode in opposite directions, so that they met each other once in a while, and paused a moment to "pass the time of day" — or rather, night.

As he rode his pony at a walk around the cattle, a cowboy continually sang or crooned softly. He might sing a cowboy melody, and many a range song has been created on trail drives. Or perhaps he might prefer a Southern love song.

He sang not only because cattle enjoy being sung to, but because the singing told the beasts where each rider was, so that they would not be surprised by his sudden appearance near them in the dark.

There was always danger that a sleeping animal thus startled might leap to its feet with a snort and a bound. That would bring others to their feet also, and might send off the whole herd in a blind stampede of galloping hoofs and clattering horns. So the cowboys sang, and the cattle were reassured and soothed, and the herd rested.

The men ate only twice a day — at night after the herd was bedded down, and before dawn when it was time to start the cattle moving again. As camp was reached toward evening, and the herd halted to graze its fill before lying down, the chuck wagon, with a fire burning brightly beside it, was a welcome sight. There the cook toiled, and as the cowboys finished their duties they dismounted, unsaddled, and walked over to take their tin plates and fill them with hot food — sometimes boiled beans and salt pork, sometimes meat with gravy, always biscuits and molasses, occasionally other simple dishes, prepared in big iron kettles called Dutch ovens. And this rough but plentiful fare the men washed down with steaming hot black coffee, drunk from tin cups.

One man, talking of trail driving long after, said, "The only kick I had driving cows up north was that I had to eat two suppers every night."

"Two suppers?" someone asked.

"Yep," he said. "One after dark and the second before sunup next morning."

This was almost true. Long before dawn the camp would be roused by a cry, "Chuck-away!" or, "Come an' get it while it's hot!"

The cook, first up each morning, had the meal ready at the fire. Then the sleeping cowboys would awaken, curse good-humoredly, roll out of their blankets — no tents were with this outfit and everyone slept in the open, rain or shine — and taking their bedrolls, toss them in the chuck wagon and eat their simple but hearty meal.

During the night the horse herd was kept near camp, but each rider always had one horse — his "night horse" in which he put special trust — saddled and bridled and picketed near where he slept, in case of stampedes or other trouble.

It was after they ate breakfast that the men got their morning mounts. This was done by forming a "rope corral." The cowboys took turns at this. A few of them stood wide apart in a big circle, with lariats stretched from hand to hand all the way around. Into this circle the ponies were driven, and it was interesting to see how the little horses seemed to recognize the series of stretched lariats as a "fence." Though they could easily break through it, they respected it, as if it were a rule of the game they were playing. Ropers — often the head remuda man was the best of the crew with a lariat — would catch the particular animals designated by each of the cowboys, who would then lead them out of the circle, saddle them, and prepare to ride them.

At this juncture excitement often occurred. Frequently a horse, when first mounted, objected. Then was seen the stirring sight of a fine rider subduing a rebellious beast, as the bronco did its very best to buck him out of the saddle.

Often as the rider swung up, the first jump of the horse came. A good horseman took it into account. He landed in the saddle, and the fight was on.

Two or three bounds forward, and the stubborn head of the pony went down. The horse "swallowed his head" as the saying was, at the same time arching his back, with a squeal.

Spectacular, jolting leaps followed, and some horses had the habit of "swapping ends" while in midair, which made them doubly hard to stay on. Often the bucking bronco would roar his hate. One old-timer said, "There is nothing more terrifying, at first, than the bawl of a maddened bronco, but you soon get used to it, for it goes on every day. You even grow to like it — if some other fellow is doing the riding."

Yells of encouragement rose from the onlooking cowboys.

"Give him the gaff, Reb!"

"That's it! Stay in your tree!"*

"Watch that fuzztail pitch!"

* Cowboy slang for saddle.

But the long, slack rider in the saddle was not shaken in his seat. With an instinct for balance as nice as that of any tightrope walker or trapeze performer, he shifted his body to each tempestuous, jolting bound of the animal beneath him. And now he took a hand in the fight. His quirt fell and his spurs bit deeply in the horse's flanks.

"Rake him! Rake him!" yelled the spectators, hugely enjoying the spectacle, which was always new to a cowboy however often he saw it.

But the pony was satisfied. The thing had ceased to be fun. One or two more "crow hops," and he suddenly seemed to forget all about bucking, and would from then on be obedient and intelligent in his work for the rest of the day.

The West had a saying, however: "Never was a horse that couldn't be rode; never was a man that couldn't be throwed." Sometimes a cowboy found himself hitting the ground. After that there was only one thing to do — catch the horse and ride him again until he decided to be good.

By this time the herd of cattle would be on its way, guided by the last of the night watchers. When these came to the cook wagon after being relieved, and ate their breakfast, the cook cleaned up the dishes, loaded everything in the wagon, hitched up his mules, and started for the next camp place.

Story by this time felt his outfit was in its routine. After those first few days, the longhorns were allowed to graze for the first three or four hours, but even as they did so they were moved in the desired direction. Presently the pace was quickened. At noon the cattle might be allowed to rest and graze, and drink if water was available. Then the drive would continue until the bedding ground was reached. An average day's drive, if there were no mishaps, was about fifteen miles.

4

BUT MISHAPS did occur.

That year, 1866, was exceptionally wet. It rained frequently, not only in the day but at night, and sleeping often was damp, cold, and uncomfortable. Sometimes the camp ground was so boggy that three men would take their bedrolls and spread their wet tarpaulins with the wet blankets on them in such a way that they could sleep in the form of a triangle, each with his head on the next man's ankles, using this means of keeping their faces out of the mud and water.

Those long rainy periods were times of danger for two reasons: the rivers and creeks were all in flood; and the chances of stampedes increased.

From Fort Worth, Nelson Story followed what was called the Sedalia Trail. The more famous Chisholm Trail came into use later when Abilene grew up as a railhead cattle market in Kansas.

The Sedalia route, which had been followed by most of the previous trail herds that spring, led northeast by way of two Indian towns, Colbert's Ferry and Boggy Depot, to Baxter Springs in the southeast corner of Kansas, and thence across Missouri to Sedalia where, presumably, cattle could be exchanged for money. Story did not intend to go to Sedalia, but he did wish to cross eastern Kansas, because a business visit to Fort Leavenworth was part of his plan in this drive, which was to go farther north than any of the others. So Baxter Springs was his first destination.

At best wild cattle were prone to stampede, and the stampede was the terror of the trail, especially a night stampede. Almost anything might set a herd off on the run — scratching a match to light a cigarette near a herd at night, or a sneeze, or even a vagrant tumbleweed rolling along in the breeze. Once, near Boggy Depot, a hen which flew cackling off her nest after laying an egg sent a thousand longhorns in a desperate and costly stampede.

Stormy nights were the worst times. One of Story's cowboys might well furnish a close-up view of such an occasion. For convenience he is called Kirby here.

Night has come down, the cook fire still flickers where the cook is doing some things in preparation for the next morning's meal. Indistinct, formless bundles here and there show where some of the men are rolled in their blankets trying to sleep, although most of them are not sleeping.

Kirby's night herd trick will start in less than an hour, so he has not even taken his bedroll out of the chuck wagon. Instead he sits talking to a friend, Buck, and smoking a cigarette waiting for his time to go on duty.

Over to the west he has seen — everyone has — a huge black cloud bank building up, lit balefully now and then with flashes of distant lightning. Occasionally a grumble of thunder comes to his ears.

The trail boss, Nelson Story, comes over. He turns and takes a look at the western sky, and then says, "Boys, you'd better cinch the saddles tight on your night horses."

By that he means that every man is likely to be in the saddle before this night is over, and Kirby, who is about to go on duty, glances at that towering black cloud with a sense of anxiety.

"Looks like a goose drownder," says Buck.

"Could be a hell wind [tornado] in that," Kirby replies, and he hopes he is wrong.

It comes time for him to take his turn with the herd. He goes over to his pony, feels the saddle cinches, and tightens them. To have a saddle turn, on a night such as this is likely to be, might mean the end of him.

Then he swings into his saddle, and his horse, knowing what he is to do, starts off for the herd, not at a canter or even a trot, but at the shuffling walk of a cow pony. The cowboy hears the herders who are on duty singing their cattle lullabies, and he starts to sing himself, maybe a cow country ballad like "Bury me not on the lone prairie." His voice may not be the best, but the cattle are not particular as long as they hear him.

The man he is to relieve pauses beside him, lounging in his saddle, before heading to camp. "Looks bad off west," he says. "Keep an eye peeled on them critters tonight."

Kirby gives a mirthless grin. "If they don't want to run, I sure ain't goin' to make them."

Then he begins his circuit of the herd. It is bedded down. That is, most of the cattle are lying down chewing their cuds, although a few restless ones may still be grazing.

A louder rumble comes from the west. A heavy thunderstorm is approaching, and the cowboy hopes, without much conviction, that it may go around him and the cattle — or that by some wild chance the herd will stay easy where it is.

He has seen the layout of the ground about the little plain where the herd was bedded while it was still daylight. And he knows it is bad — cut up in crooked ditches, gullies, and dry washes, and studded here and there with prairie dog villages, acres of little mounds on which a horse may stumble in the dark, with holes just big enough to take a horse's foot and break his leg as he is carried on by his own momentum.

Should the cattle stampede, Kirby knows he will have to ride his pony at the dead run, and though this is the mount of his string he trusts most, even the surest-footed horse may trip and fall in the pitch darkness. If he is thrown there will be wildly stampeding cattle around him, behind, before, on each side. And to be caught under a rush like that is death.

The storm continues to approach, the great cloud looms higher and higher, and the first scudding forerunning smaller clouds pass overhead. The night has been hot and muggy, but still. Kirby knows, however, that there will be wind in this storm.

Now the vast cloud seems to crouch over him, blotting out the stars, and the air becomes filled with electricity. All at once he begins to see what appear to be small luminous bulbs of light on the tips of the horns of some of the cattle. This is what is called "fox fire," but it is the same thing a sailor knows as "St. Elmo's fire" when it appears at the ends of masts and spars at sea. The flickering blue or yellow lights in the herd give a very weird effect.

The cowboy continues riding around the herd, singing his song, hoping against hope, although he feels already that "hell's about to pop," as he phrases it.

Now he sees a bad sign in the herd. Some of the cattle begin to rise, standing tense and trembling. Others seem to crouch, their legs drawn up as if ready for a sudden spring.

Suddenly the whole dark world blazes in the white light of a blinding lightning flash, accompanied by a terrific crash of thunder.

In that instant the whole herd goes, thousands of hoofs drumming at once, horns clashing, the cattle bellowing with fear, bounding off into the darkness which now has become even blacker because of the heavy rain that begins to sweep across the night landscape driven by a chilling wind.

For Kirby there is only one move possible — he goes

with the herd. He is among the leaders of the cattle, which means that the others are behind him. He must stay ahead.

At the same time he knows that every man in the camp, except the cook, is riding. There has been no sleeping as that storm built up. At the lightning bolt, the thunderclap, and the roar of the cattle's flight, the cowboys, swearing but wide awake, leap into the saddles of their tethered night horses and without orders set off after the flying longhorns.

Off to one side Kirby sees the flash, although he does not hear the report in the tumult, of a six-shooter fired in the air. One of his fellow herd riders, also caught in the stampede, is trying to turn the animals.

But there is no heading off this blind, terrible rush. He knows it, and he grimly keeps his six-shooter in its holster. The only hope is to go on with the stampede at the top speed of his horse.

The pony he is riding knows this as well as he does. The little horse's legs drum out a cadence, the wet dark earth streams beneath him, and his pace increases with the growing thunder of hoofs.

Kirby feels his saddle strings stream behind, the mane of his pony whips his bridle hand. Dimly he is conscious of a shallow wash, now slippery and with water in its bottom. But his brave little mount plunges through its rocks and mud recklessly, to the firmer ground on the other side.

All at once the pony stumbles slightly. The cowboy realizes he is in the very middle of an extensive prairie dog town, with its holes like pitfalls and probabilities of broken legs. Then they are beyond. His pony has skipped and dodged through successfully.

He is beginning to draw ahead of the foremost cattle, which he must do if he is to turn them. His horse extends himself with a snort as if he actually enjoys this perilous race.

Suddenly they come to a jarring stop, and Kirby finds himself staring over his pony's head down into a gully both steep and deep. The little horse has seen it just in time and come to one of those wonderful stops that only a cow pony can execute.

Almost at once he turns, and finding a less precipitous crossing, scrambles down and over. He is just in the wink of time, too, for the cattle come plunging after like a cataract over a dam, and it is only a wonder that some of them are not killed — although few, apparently, are injured.

On race the man and horse. By this time they have been running at the top speed of the pony for several miles. The herd has strung out behind, the fastest long-legged steers ahead, the cows and calves and bulls farther back.

In the darkness the cowboy senses another rider toward his right. It is Buck, also on the night herd, and they swing their mounts over toward each other.

"Maybe we can start 'em circling here," Kirby gasps.

"Let's swing 'em left," Buck answers.

Now the two of them, revolvers spurting fire toward the heavens, try to get the running cattle to change direction. At first it is hard to do, but both the cow ponies are experienced. Still at utmost speed they gradually manage to turn the leading steers.

As the leaders swing in a wide arc, the others follow

them, and other cowboys are coming up behind to help. It is still raining heavily, although the front of the storm with its lightning and thunder has passed on over.

The herd, under the urging of the riders, begins to circle; the circle gradually grows smaller. At last the cattle are in a dense mob — in the language of the cowboys, "milling" — and can now be controlled.

Morning finds Kirby and his friends a long way from camp, and they begin to move the herd toward it. Always during a stampede, some of the cattle, in little bands ranging sometimes up to a hundred in numbers, manage to break away from the rest. These must be hunted when daylight comes, so more time is lost.

With the earliest daylight, as the herd, now tamed for a time, works back on the long trail it has run during the night, Nelson Story, who has ridden as long and hard as any of his crew, counts noses. Two men are missing.

There is deep worry over this, for many a cowboy has lost his life in such stampedes, being thrown by his falling horse and trampled underfoot by fear-crazed cattle.

But about noon the two missing riders appear — driving before them a bunch of cattle they rounded

up after it broke away from the main herd. Perhaps
Story has lost a few cattle, dead or wandering, but on
the whole he feels lucky that things turned out as well
as they did.

This stampede is over, and nobody is happier than
Kirby, the cowboy who was in front of it all the way!

During that long march north this sort of thing happened again and again. No wonder the men grew
gaunt and weary almost to the limit of endurance.

"I might as well trade my bedroll for a lantern and be done with it," grumbled one of the men.

There was actual danger, sometimes, that a cow-puncher might fall asleep in his saddle, with the possibility of falling off and injuring himself. To combat this, they used what was known as a "rouser" — a little tobacco juice, placed on the insides of the eyelids which smarted painfully and inflamed the eyes, but kept away drowsiness for the time being.

Next to a stampede, crossing a herd over a large river was the biggest problem. There were no bridges, and in that very wet season of 1866 all the rivers were high, some of them at flood stage. The only way to get the cattle across was to make them swim, and this was a feat difficult, exciting, and dangerous.

Story and his men put their herd across the Red River, the Washita, the Canadian, the North Canadian, the Cimarron, and the Arkansas — six big rivers, all "booming" as the saying was when a stream was bank-full, with angry waters rushing at full tide. There were also smaller streams, some of them treacherous with quicksands.

Both courage and coolness were required to get a herd across a swirling, muddy river, with debris of various kinds floating on it, such as uprooted trees, logs, even the dead bodies of drowned animals. Any failure might bring heavy losses in cattle and perhaps death to cowboys.

Story's riders knew when they were approaching a river, but the cattle at first did not. What was to be done must be done decisively and quickly, without giving the longhorns time to realize what was ahead.

As the river was neared, the point riders took special care to keep the leaders of the herd moving briskly, while behind them the swing men and drag riders hurried the rest of the cattle, keeping them bunched and following as compactly as possible.

All at once the leading steers would find themselves at the bank of the river. They might try to hesitate. If so, there were shrill cries, and cowboys used the ends of their ropes to spur action. In any case, whether they wished it or not, the leaders were so crowded by the rest of the cattle following blindly that they were forced to plunge in.

Next a cowboy on a swimming horse struck out boldly ahead, toward the far shore. The leaders, in the water, seeing that they could not go back, instinctively followed the swimming horse and man in front.

Behind them successive ranks of cattle plunged in, "crowded," as the cowboys said; and these struck out after their leaders. The whole idea was to keep the herd moving. No open water should intervene between the bank and the cattle already swimming, and as long as there were others of their kind near at hand in the river, the animals seemed to follow their example.

Other cowboys entered the water, swimming their horses along with the herd, while those still on the bank shouted and flailed with their quirts or lariat ropes, to keep the tail of the herd moving forward in a mass. A continuous stream of cattle was soon going across.

Longhorns swimming a river looked strange, for

their bodies were entirely below the surface as they swam. Horned heads, with starting eyes and flaring nostrils, were all that could be seen on the current.

"Like a thousand rocking chairs floating on the water," grinned one cowboy.

But suddenly there was trouble ahead. Something — a whirlpool, or a floating log, or a carcass carried down the stream — had broken the continuous line of swimming cattle. Some of the longhorns were turning away from the opposite shore, as if they would swim back from where they came.

This was a moment of danger. If they were not

straightened out the cattle would soon be in a hopeless tangle and many would drown.

To meet this crisis the nearest cowpunchers swam their horses right into the mass of wide-spreading horns, threshing bodies, and churning hoofs. With yells and curses and lashing quirts, they tried to start the herd swimming once more in the right direction.

In the midst of this watery confusion, one man was unhorsed. He disappeared under the water in the midst of a bunch of swimming steers. His companions looked anxiously for him.

A moment later his head reappeared, and there was a cheer. He had caught hold of a steer's tail.

"Ride it out, Johnny!" yelled his friends.

The cattle had by this time been untangled, and the herd was crossing smoothly once more, but Johnny's steer, feeling the man hanging to his tail, put forth a really strenuous effort. He swam with great surges, so that Johnny's head was under water as much as it was out.

Nevertheless he clung to his hold, and the steer towed him to the bank, where he clambered out, muddy and soaked to the skin. The steer, finding his tail no longer grasped, galloped away to join the other cattle already across.

Johnny's friends, in sheer relief, laughed and unmercifully teased him.

"Johnny looked just like a catfish!" said one.

"Or a yalligator," said another.

"More like a mud turtle," chimed in a third.

Johnny only grinned. He knew he had been very lucky, for many trail drivers were killed trying to swim among the frantically churning hoofs and horns. His horse, which landed downstream, was captured. The chuck wagon was floated across on a makeshift raft, the mules swimming. Another river had been passed.

Another form of mishap, exasperating and time-killing, should be recorded here. Occasionally in the smaller streams quicksand was encountered. The heaviest steers, which were the most valuable, of course were the ones usually caught first.

When an animal found itself beginning to sink, it became panic-stricken, and its struggles only sent it deeper into the treacherous sand, until it was in up to the level of its body. The body gave enough resistance so that it sank no farther, but it was hopelessly bogged. If it were not gotten out, it would starve there, or a rise of the stream would drown it.

Sometimes as many as ten or twenty cattle would be

trapped at one time in this manner. There was only one way to get them out. The cowboys would wade out to dig the bogged steer loose from the merciless grasp of the quicksand.

As long as a man kept moving he was all right, but if he halted he would begin to sink. Knowing this the cowboys did not stay long in one place, but continually changed their footing.

The steer was helpless, but angry. They fastened a heavy rope about his horns, which was taken to solid ground where several cowboys could, when needed, fasten their lariats to it in order to pull.

Meantime those in the stream bed dug around the animal with their hands, trying to free his legs, until they could turn him on his side. With the legs free the horsemen on the bank, each pony hauling on the lariat fastened to the heavy rope, would go into action.

A great heave, and the steer would slide out in a humiliating position on his side, until he could scramble to his feet on dry land.

Then the fun began. Usually a steer was enraged, under the mistaken belief that the men had been playing some kind of a practical joke on him, and would charge the nearest thing in sight.

Once a big black bull, when freed, pursued a cowboy on his pony until they chanced to pass the chuck wagon. At once the savage animal whirled toward the wagon, horns lowered, tail up, bellowing in fury.

The cook had plenty to worry about. That bull might gore and even kill one or more mules, or he might smash a wheel by driving into the spokes. Rising to his feet in the wagon, the cook cracked his long mule whip, starting his mules ahead.

In his charge, the bull missed the rear of the wagon by inches, but at once he turned and pursued it. Away went the wagon, bouncing over bumps, sometimes all four wheels in the air at once, while the cook "poured the whip" into his mules which now, thoroughly scared, were galloping, the bull close behind the wagon they drew.

Several mounted cowboys made efforts to cut the bull off from the wagon, or attract his attention to something else. But that bull saw in the chuck wagon the symbol of all the indignities he had suffered, and he pursued relentlessly as if determined to smash it.

Around and around the cook drove the chuck wagon, in wide circles, hoping the cowboys would stop his mad pursuer. The riders tried, but they were laughing so hard at the cook's efforts to escape, that they did not do much good.

At length the bull gave up the chase, and turned on the horsemen, whose ponies easily kept out of his way. Finally, in sheer baffled fury, unable to get at anything else, the great black bull charged a red clay bank and began hooking it with his horns. For several minutes he vented his rage in this manner, sending the red clay flying in every direction and covering his back and head with it.

Meantime the chuck wagon found a sand dune to hide behind, and when the bull had revenged himself enough on the clay bank, he looked around, did not see the original object of his fury, gave a final defiant

bellow, and trotted off toward the herd some distance away. Once there, he became tractable once more.

The cowboys were almost sick with laughter. The cook began to receive their gibes.

"What's the matter, Cookie, did you think you was drivin' a chariot?" asked one.

"No, Cookie thought he was swinging a battery of artillery around in maneuvers," said another.

"Sure handicapped himself by ridin' in that wagon," a third added. "He could have done a lot better on foot."

"I'll bet Cookie could make antelopes look like they was growed fast to the ground, if he was runnin' with that bull after him," a fourth tormentor said.

But the cook had the last word. He gave a bleak grin. "I didn't see none of you heroes get down off your horses to engage in foot races with that animal," he said. "Furthermore, you-all notice I saved your grub. I don't know why I went to all that trouble. And another thing: From now on you wags better be mighty polite with me. Fact is, I think that startin' right away, I'm goin' to feed you-all nothin' but beans and sowbelly for the rest of this drive."

That ended the laughter. Every cowboy knew how unlucky it was to be in the bad graces of the cook. A man could find himself having the worst of it every time he got his plate served when he wanted to eat.

But in this case the cook could see the joke as well as anyone, and he relented. His cooking did not get worse, and he even showed that he held no grudges by digging out a carefully hoarded bag of dried peaches, and making a dessert for them that night.

All in all, Nelson Story's crew up to now had been lucky. Not a man of them had been killed or injured, either in stampedes or the crossing of swollen rivers. The cattle losses were small. But a long road still lay ahead of the outfit.

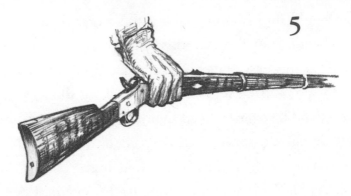

THE TRAIL DRIVERS had no real idea of what Nelson Story intended to do. He was reserved, almost short, in his speech; and his men by this time had come to respect him and ask few questions.

As one of his cowpunchers said long after, "He wasn't 'bad,' but he was the kind of a man you could spend a heap of your spare time leavin' alone."

The Texas cowboys probably thought that all he wanted to do was get the cattle to the market at Sedalia. But he was following the Sedalia route, first because it was the best known trail from Fort Worth northward, and second because it was the most direct way to Fort Leavenworth, Kansas, and from there to the Oregon Trail, which led westward to where the Bozeman Trail cut across the wild Wyoming country toward Montana and his home.

Day after day he drove his cattle — and his men. The trail drivers did not have enough sleep, but he slept less than any of them — in brief snatches only. If he rolled into a blanket on the ground at night to catch some very badly needed rest, he always woke if the night noises of the longhorns changed tone, or the wind shifted to a direction that might indicate a storm, or the coyotes yowled too close to camp — the little wolves liked to creep in and chew up leather lariats or bridles — or when the sound of hoofs or footsteps came near.

They began crossing the country of the Cherokees, and Choctaws, and Creeks. These were fairly civilized Indians, many of them farmers and stock raisers. At first they did not object to an occasional herd passing through their reservations, but when, in 1866, more than a quarter of a million wild-eyed longhorns came up the trail, breaking down fences, trampling growing crops, eating every bit of grass in sight, and frequently causing the Indians' stock to run away, the tribes objected.

So one morning Nelson Story saw a group of mounted men ahead, and made out that they were Indians — Cherokees, evidently. These people understood the laws of the white man, and they wanted to protect themselves.

They told Story that he was trespassing with his "Wo-haws."*

Next, with poker faces, the Cherokees demanded a toll of ten cents a head on every animal passing through their lands. They told Story that he could take one trail, and one only, and indicated it — the trail already followed by many herds and almost completely bare of grass. Finally, they wanted to ride through the herd to cut out any of their own cattle that might have mingled with it.

Story was a just man. Ten cents a head for a thousand cattle — though he did not now have that many — came to a hundred dollars, a lot of money to him just then. Yet he believed the Indians deserved it and allowed them to count his herd and paid accordingly.

Story also was willing for the Indians to recover any stock of theirs that might have got mixed with his longhorns. So he let them look through his herd, and they found few if any with their brands.

---

* The first cattle the Indians saw were work oxen, pulling wagons, and the commands given to direct these teams were "Whoa" for "Stop," "Haw" for "Left," and "Gee" for "Right." The first two of these commands, simplified to "Wo-haw," became the Indian name for cattle — all kinds of cattle.

But he absolutely refused to take his cattle over a worn-out trail where there was no grass. Those animals meant too much to him to be starved to death on the way.

So, having done what he thought was justice in meeting the demands of the Indians, he simply ordered his men to start moving the herd. The Indians had firearms, and neither Story nor his men "pulled iron" (as the West termed the drawing of a six-shooter).

But the red men looked at the trail boss's stern face, and the hard visages of his crew, and they decided not to oppose these tough, daredevil riders, who could be most dangerous.

The cattle took a trail to the left of the main route, and found sufficient grazing to carry them along.

They had passed the Indian Nations, but up ahead there were men of a different type who might spell serious trouble.

That year the cattlemen who took herds north to Kansas had met bitter disappointment, of which Story had heard rumors at Fort Worth. On the lower border of Kansas, cattle were being stopped, their drivers threatened, some even shot. And the herds piled up like water behind a dam in the Indian Territory, until they ate off all the grass and there were fearful losses from starvation.

This at first was because the farmers of Kansas and Missouri objected to having Texas cattle driven through their territory. They said, with truth, that Texas cattle spread what was then called "Texas fever," or "Spanish fever," a fatal disease, among their own stock. Nobody then knew that cattle ticks, brought north by cattle from the brush country, caused this infection of animals — unless they were immune, as all Texas cattle were.

When it was found that the ticks caused the fever, the remedy was simple. All cattle were driven through deep "dipping" chutes, filled with tick-killing chemicals, and the ticks were dead. But this knowledge came too late to help the trail drivers of 1866, and unfortunately the honest objections of the farmers were made a pretext by men who were not honest, and who were deadly if they were opposed. These were the so-called "Jayhawkers."

During the Civil War bands of bloody and destructive guerrillas scourged the Kansas-Missouri border. Those from Kansas were called Jayhawkers, those from Missouri Bushwhackers. They were shifty and murderous bandits — outlaws really — for the real soldiers and the governments of both North and South disowned them and hunted them down whenever they could.

Since the war these lawless men had slim pickings, but they quickly saw in the opposition of honest farmers to the passage of the trail herds, an ideal chance to use their shady tactics.

Heavily armed bands of them met the cattle drivers below the border, in the guise of "honest farmers," and abused and insulted the cowboys in hope that they would resist so there could be a pretext for murdering them and stealing their herds. Sometimes hotheaded Texans went down fighting, and some few Jayhawkers — as the Texans called all these guerrillas — were buried after sudden battles in which six-shooters barked.

But usually the trail drivers, outnumbered, swallowed the abuse and turned back, holding their cattle below the border, hoping for a change that might let them finish their drives.

Nelson Story's outfit reached these starving herds, and he talked to some of the trail bosses, so he knew that men had been tied to trees and mercilessly whipped, and others killed for resisting the Jayhawker bandits. He learned also that the Jayhawkers could be

bought off for two or three dollars a head — a flagrant blackmail.

In spite of this he continued right on toward the Kansas border.

When he neared it, he and his men saw a compact body of riders come out from a clump of trees where they were camped, and spreading out, gallop toward him. As they neared him, he could see that they amply justified all the bitter things the Texas cattlemen had said about them.

Up they rode, a swaggering, dirty, bewhiskered, criminal gang, every man heavily armed with six-shooters and rifle. The leader raised an arm, as a signal for his men to halt, while he rode forward. Right in front of Story's horse he reined up, and the trail boss found himself looking at as ugly a specimen of depraved outlawry as he had ever seen.

"You the boss of this outfit?" asked the man.

"I am," said Story.

"We're agents for the Granger's Association,"* said the Jayhawker.

"Well?" said Story, who knew this was a lie.

"We're turnin' back all Texas longhorns on account of the Texas fever," said the man.

Nelson Story looked them over. There were enough of them, and they were deadly enough, to wipe out his cowboys if it came to a battle. But he said nothing. He merely looked the Jayhawker chief in the eye.

After a time this scrutiny seemed to make the Jayhawker nervous. He spoke again, and indicated that he "would listen to a proposition."

Story was aware that the "proposition" referred to was that he should bribe his way through by paying these robbers two or three dollars a head on his cattle. But he had no intention of paying any bribes. In fact,

---

* The Granger's Association was an organization of legitimate farmers in both Kansas and Missouri.

at this time he first revealed a part, at least, of his great plan.

Turning to his men he saw at once that if he said "Fight," they would only too willingly obey, even if every one of them went down. His usually good-humored cowboys could be dangerous when they felt themselves insulted or bullied. Their faces were as grim as his own. They were just reckless enough, and loyal enough to him, that the merest spark might set off a bloody explosion.

His face did not change as he quietly ordered, "Turn the herd back."

Some of his men looked incredulous. They did not think he would back down. But he was the boss. They swung their horses around to obey his command.

If any of them had doubts about him, those doubts disappeared that night. He directed that the herd be headed west, below the Kansas border, and *away* from the Sedalia market.

Then he told them where he intended to drive those cattle. There were thousands of people in Montana Territory, and those thousands had to have meat. He intended to take his herd there.

What he was proposing to them was a drive un-precedented in cattle history. They had thought they were nearing the end of the drive, but now, if they figured right, they were less than a third of the distance they must go.

It was a tremendous challenge that he was presenting to them, and it may have been a nervous moment for him as he waited for their answer. If so he did not show it, and he did not have to wait long for the reply.

The greatest proof of the way he had won their loyalty was that when he informed them where he was going, not one of them asked for his pay and quit. They looked at each other, those bronzed riders, and their lips tightened and eyes narrowed as they thought of the dangers ahead. But most of them had been soldiers, and Nelson Story had proved that he was a leader. They believed in him, and like soldiers they obeyed him.

All through the dark hours the herd moved west, Story riding like a shadow among shadows, up and down the line, speaking to each of his riders, giving them confidence as they moved the cattle out of reach of the Jayhawkers.

The longhorns trailed west for a few days, and then turned north, according to the best information available, along the Arkansas River to the vicinity of present-day Wichita, Kansas, and then straight north for the Nebraska line and the Oregon Trail. This route lay through an area that had as yet few settlements, where the grass was good and the streams easy to cross.

But Nelson Story himself, after getting his cattle headed in the right direction, and giving instructions to his men, left the herd and rode alone straight north for Fort Leavenworth, which was on the Missouri River some distance east of the line his outfit was taking.

It was at Fort Leavenworth that he had begun his own western career ten years before, in 1856. It was at Fort Leavenworth that he met and married Ellen Trent, who now was waiting for him at Virginia City, Montana. He knew wagons and wagon driving, and he knew people at the fort and at the nearby town, and he had his letter of credit with which he intended to add something in addition to the cattle herd he was driving to Montana.

At Fort Leavenworth he bought three wagons with their ox teams — four yoke to the wagon — and he loaded them with groceries, goods, and articles of various kinds, with which he hoped to stock a store when he reached his destination. Then he hired three veteran bullwhackers to drive the wagons.

Bullwhackers were a class by themselves. They feared nothing, their language was unprintable, and they could handle the sometimes perverse oxen as if they could think with the beasts themselves. So expert were they with their twenty-foot-long bullwhips that they could, at will, flick a fly off an ox twenty feet away without touching him — or, if necessary, take a square inch of hide out of him. They were proud of their trade, and since Nelson Story had once been a bullwhacker himself, they were ready to join him.

At this place also he picked up another hand, a Canadian youth named Tom Thompson, who was to prove so reliable and capable that in later years Story made him foreman of his cattle ranch, and even named his second son for him. With these acquisitions, the trail boss started west to meet his outfit on its march to the Platte River valley.

Up the Platte ran the Oregon Trail, and at Fort Laramie, in Wyoming, the Bozeman Trail branched off. This route was blazed by Story's friend John Bozeman in 1863. In general it angled northwest from Fort Laramie, through the country of the wild and ferocious Sioux and their allies, until it reached the Yellowstone River, which it followed until it struck out for Virginia City.

The Bozeman Trail had become very dangerous lately, because the Indians resented the fact that it crossed their buffalo country and drove the game away. They had therefore begun to attack everyone who traveled on it.

Nevertheless, Story determined to drive his cattle to his home country by that route. Before the Indians stopped traffic on it, he knew that Bozeman had taken several wagon trains up that trail, and he believed that if Bozeman could take wagons along it, he also could take his wagons, as well as his herd.

One other thing that he bought at Fort Leavenworth should be mentioned — thirty rifles. They were brand-new, just invented and perfected — Remingtons, with what was known as the "rolling block."

In that day this rifle was remarkable for its rapidity of fire. It loaded at the breech, was simple, strong, and as nearly foolproof as a gun could be. To load it, the hammer was cocked, and the solid breechblock rolled straight back with the thumb. Then the cartridge was inserted, the block rolled back, and the weapon was ready to fire.

MONT.

VIRGINIA CITY

Yellowstone River

Big Horn R.

Tongue R.

Powder R.

WYO.

FORT
PHIL
KEARNY

Missouri

FORT
LARAMIE

North Platte R.

COL.

South Platte R.

NEB.

River

Platte R.

KAN.

Arkansas

River

WICHITA

TEX.

Cimarron R.

Canadian R.

OKLA.

Red R.

Arkansas R.

Nelson Story's
Route

FORT WORTH

It was not a repeating rifle, but it was the fastest thing yet developed in single-shot rifles. In the hands of an expert the Remington rolling-block could be fired seventeen times in a minute, almost as fast as the early lever-action repeating rifles that came in later.

Nelson Story was the first actually to put the Remington to active use. When he found the thirty rifles, just arrived at Fort Leavenworth, he tried one out and immediately bought the entire consignment for his men and himself. He also laid in an abundant supply of cartridges — these rifles were of .50 caliber, and ammunition of this size could be bought at arms stores in quantities.

In the East, Remingtons sold at about thirty-five dollars apiece, but prices were much higher at Fort Leavenworth. Story may have paid as much as one hundred dollars each for the rifles he bought — which meant a new outlay of $3000, not counting the cost of the ammunition. But he thought the investment wise, and events were to prove him right.

With his bull-wagons and rifles, he intercepted his outfit heading for the Oregon Trail. There was a yelling welcome from his grinning men, and one of those wagons had a special consignment of eatables and perhaps drinkables. The whole crew enjoyed a feast, and the men, used to muzzle-loading guns, inspected their new weapons with delight. After they gave the Remingtons a thorough tryout, and found that they shot true, had long range, and worked with — to them — unbelievable speed, they were ready for anything. The new rapid-fire rifles gave them confidence to face any risk.

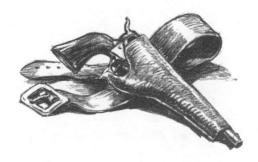

THOSE RISKS which they faced were certainly very great.

At Fort Leavenworth, Story heard news that might have caused most men to give up any idea of trying to reach Montana that year, especially with a herd of cattle.

Fighting Indians — the great Sioux Nation, and its allies, the Cheyennes, Arapahoes, and Blackfoot — were on the warpath far more fiercely than ever before. The cause of this was that although the red men had forbidden the use of the Bozeman Trail, the government was determined to keep it open, and was building forts to guard it.

The previous June, Colonel Henry M. Carrington, with a regiment of infantry, some cavalry and artillery, and a long train of supply wagons, had been sent to build those forts. He arrived at Fort Laramie, where the Bozeman Trail branched off from the Oregon Trail, on June 14, at the precise time when a treaty commission was trying to persuade the Sioux to agree peacefully to permit the road to be used.

Red Cloud, a tall, imposing-looking savage, with a deeply lined face, was on the platform talking with the commissioners when Carrington rode up. Instantly Red Cloud made a dramatic gesture.

Pointing at the silver eagles on Carrington's shoulder straps (a colonel's insignia of rank), the Sioux chief cried out:

"He is the white eagle who has come to steal a road through the Indian's land!"

With that he leaped from the platform and, followed by many of the Sioux, left the fort. Since he was one of the principal leaders of that warlike people, the others soon joined him, the treaty failed, and Red Cloud became the great chief in the war that followed.

Even before this occurrence the Sioux had proved their fighting ability. In the previous year, 1865, three strong military expeditions sent against them were forced to retire from the mountain country. They were attacked, their horses were stolen in night raids,

and they ran out of rations. When they returned, their commander, General Patrick E. Connor, reported concerning the Bozeman Trail:

"There will be no more travel on that road until the government takes care of the Indians. There is plenty of firewood, water, and game, but the Indians won't let you use them."

This report had much to do with the decision to build forts along the trail.

When the Indians departed from Fort Laramie, and all hope of peaceful agreement went with them, Carrington started his march up the Bozeman Trail after them. He stopped and strengthened a fort built by Connor on the Powder River, which had been named Fort Connor. Carrington renamed it Fort Reno, after a Union general killed in the Civil War, and left a small garrison there.

Then he marched on with the rest of his command, because he was under orders to build two more forts. One of these, named Fort Phil Kearny, was begun on Big Piney Creek, at the foot of the towering Big Horn Mountains, just below the northern border of Wyoming. The second, Fort C. F. Smith, was started on the banks of the Big Horn River, just above the Wyoming border in Montana Territory. These posts also were named after Civil War generals killed in battle.

The theory was that those three forts, Reno, Phil Kearny, and C. F. Smith, all of them overlooking the Bozeman Trail, would be enough to keep the route to the mining country open. But the government did not yet know the fierceness of the Indians.

The Sioux were furious. Red Cloud vowed he would have those forts destroyed,* and he was backed by some famous chiefs: Crazy Horse, the greatest fighter the Sioux ever produced; Black Shield and High Backbone, both Sioux; and noted Cheyenne like Dull Knife, Little Wolf, Yellow Nose, and others.

In the beginning, the Indians placed both Fort Phil Kearny and Fort C. F. Smith in a state of siege. This does not mean they formally invested the forts with earthworks, as in a regular siege. Instead they planted everywhere around the posts their hidden war parties.

The soldiers found that their foes never seemed to sleep. If a herder strayed from his guard, he was cut off and killed. If a sentry exposed himself on the

* To look forward, Red Cloud kept that vow of his. Before this war, called the Red Cloud War, was over, the government withdrew its troops from the Sioux country and the Indians burned to the ground the offending posts.

palisade during a moonlit night, a bullet from the bush laid him low. If a detachment of soldiers set forth without considerable numbers, it straightway found itself fighting for its life.

Along the headwaters of the Little Goose River and Tongue River, northwest of Fort Phil Kearny, the Sioux themselves later said they had a thousand tepees, which could mean from 7000 to 10,000 Indians of all ages and both sexes, at least 2000 of whom were warriors, since all but the women, children, and aged could and would fight.

Those hordes of hostile savages within striking distance of Fort Phil Kearny were the greatest force of fighting men the Sioux had hitherto assembled; and the greatest they would ever assemble until they met and defeated two strong army forces, one under Crook, the other under Custer, ten years later, in 1876.

There were constant raids, battles, ambushes, and skirmishes, and many lives of both white men and Indians were lost in this fighting, the soldiers getting none the best of it. Around Fort Phil Kearny, from August 1, 1866, to December 31 of the same year, the Sioux killed one hundred and fifty-four men at or near the post, and wounded many others. In addition to these, white men were slain all up and down the trail.

Nelson Story was aware of these things. But he was a man of unusual determination, and he took two factors into account. It was September, the beginning of fall, when he and his outfit reached the Oregon Trail and started westward along it for Fort Laramie, where the Bozeman Trail began. Winter came early in the mountains, and he knew the Indians were less active in cold weather than in warm weather; also that they might be busy now getting in their winter's supply of meat in the great buffalo hunts in which they always engaged.

He pinned some of his hopes on that, but he put even greater faith in those Remington rifles, and in the men who now carried them, each with a leather rifle scabbard hung from his saddle.

The Union Pacific Railroad, which would join with the Central Pacific from the West, and provide the nation with a transcontinental line, was being built in 1866. Story's dusty, noisy procession of cattle, horsemen, and wagons, more than a mile long, paralleled the railroad right-of-way, which ran as far as Grand Island, Nebraska Territory, the railhead that winter. From there the outfit was left on its own.

Following the south bank of the river, a crossing of
the South Platte was made near its junction with the
North Platte. This was not difficult since the river was
low, but the North Platte was full and rapid.

Thus far the Texans had seen only the wild beasts
of their own country — the inevitable coyotes that
shrieked around the camp every night; occasional lobo
wolves, with deeper howls, that must be watched, for
they could pull down a calf if given a chance; the little
wild pigs called javelinas or peccaries; deer sometimes;
and very rarely a quick glimpse of a cougar in the
distance.

But now they were in territory where great antlered elk could still be seen. Antelope, speediest of all running creatures, were frequent spectacles. Deer were to be found, of course. So elk, antelope, and deer steaks and roasts furnished agreeable variations to the camp diet.

But there were other animals also. Black bears might sometimes be encountered along the rivers, and later, in the mountains the huge and dangerous grizzly bears might dispute the trail. Most spectacular of all were the buffalo which occasionally were seen. Buffalo were a source of danger, for they could stampede cattle. There was something so impressive and menacing about the appearance of a huge old buffalo bull that the cattle went out of their minds in panic. A bear might set the cattle running, too, if one appeared unexpectedly.

So Story sent a couple of men riding out ahead of the herd to chase such animals off the trail, or shoot them if they did not give way.

Big lobo wolves, of course, were still about, and coyote were everywhere. Prairie dog settlements were many and widespread. These animals helped to provide interest for the men in the long and rather monotonous march up the North Platte to Fort Laramie, which was situated on the south bank of that stream.

Fort Laramie! A fur trading post once, then a military fort, it had a long and interesting history. It had seen Indian wars, the great rush of gold miners to California and land-seekers to Oregon, the march of the Mormons to Utah; and it had been visited by countless famous men — authors, painters, soldiers, scientists of every description. To Story and his crew its chief interest was the fact that from there the Bozeman Trail — and the real Indian country — began, the wildest, roughest, most dangerous area in America.

When Nelson Story paid his respects to the officers at Fort Laramie, they shook their heads. "It's crazy," they said. "You can't travel up through that hostile country with a slow-moving herd. You'll be seen — you can't escape it — and you'll be easy prey for the Indians. Sioux war parties have been busy all summer and fall taking scalps up and down that trail."

Story listened. "Well," he said at last, "I'm going to give it a try, anyway."

"You go at your own risk," said the commandant. "The army can't spare enough soldiers to protect you."

Some of the men in the outfit talked together a little nervously. "Thousands of Sioux up ahead," they said to each other. "They kill you. Or, if they capture you alive, they torture you to death —"

But all at once Nelson Story himself was among them.

"Get the herd moving," he said, as calmly as if no danger existed ahead for any of them. Then he added:

"Think it over, boys. I believe you'll see that in plain fact the odds are on our side and *against* the Indians. The best they've got in guns are old muzzle-loader muskets, and not too many of them —and a lot of those are out of order, because Indians are careless that way. Most of them have nothing better than bows and arrows.

"Now, what have we got? The best rapid-fire rifles in the world! We can get off ten shots while a Sioux is shooting and reloading his musket once. And our rifles outrange theirs. You boys who were in military service have seen fighting a lot more murderous than any we may have with a wandering band of savages!"*

---

* This actually was an underestimation of the fighting prowess of the Indians. Guns or no, they were deadly. When later the Sioux and Cheyennes fought Captain William J. Fetterman's command near Fort Phil Kearny, and killed every man in it, of the eighty-one dead white men only four were killed by Indian bullets. Two others, Captains Fetterman and Brown, committed suicide by shooting themselves to prevent capture. All the others were slain by arrows, lances, war clubs, tomahawks, or knives. But this was in the future, and neither Story nor anybody else could foretell it.

He was a leader, and he knew how to appeal to the pride of his men. They were, after all, fighting men, among whom courage was taken for granted. And those Remingtons were mighty splendid shooting irons. Besides, there had grown up a great loyalty and belief in Nelson Story. "We'd have followed him to hell," said one of his men years later.

"Let's go!" exclaimed the cowpunchers.

And so the sullen, red-eyed longhorns were started swimming across one more river, the North Platte. The wagons were crossed over by the ferry at Fort Laramie, but the best swimming place was some miles below the fort, where several islands offered resting places for cattle in their swim. Men had to be stationed on these islands, to keep the cattle from staying there too long. The middle channel of the river was nearly a hundred yards wide, but this was nothing at all for Story's longhorns who had crossed so many streams they seemed almost to know what to do without any direction.

By nightfall the whole herd was over, without mishap. It was allowed to graze while the cowboys ate supper near the chuck wagon, which with the ox wagons reached the outfit after being ferried over upstream. There were now two new men to get acquainted with. They were from Indiana, where they had tried farming, and decided they would go to the mining country instead. Their names were John B. Catlin and Steve Grover, and both had been soldiers in the Union army during the recent war. They had a wagon, a mule team, and a pair of riding horses, and they had been waiting for some big outfit to join, for protection. Both Catlin* and Grover took orders without question from Nelson Story when he gave them permission to come with him, and they proved to be brave and valuable men. There is no record that these two Union boys and the Confederate veterans in the outfit were ever anything but friends and fighting comrades from the first.

Story already had a grave new problem to consider. The dry nature of the country was noticeable. The North Platte had its sources in the mountains, which gave it plenty of water, but all the streams, or rather dry beds on this high plateau, had no source but occasional rains or snows. Names of these "creeks" had a monotonous tone: Dry Fork, Sand Creek, Wind

---

* Catlin was called Major Catlin in his later years. It was perhaps an honorary title, for he was a very young man at the close of the war, and he once spoke of having been "three years on the skirmish line in the Civil War." Army majors were not usually sent on skirmish-line duty.

Creek, Alkali Creek. The trail boss had been told that
after the Cheyenne River was passed, he had an
eighty-mile drive before him, to reach the next water
in the Powder River.

He said little about this at first. The drivers rode
about the herd as it plodded along. Behind came the
wagons — Story's three, loaded with provisions and
goods, each pulled by eight oxen guided by whiskered,
tobacco-spitting, whip-cracking bullwhackers; the
mule team with the wagon of the Indiana boys; and
the chuck wagon. The cook did not drive ahead of
the herd these days, and Story also stayed with his
men, because it was dangerous to get very far from the
outfit with Indians likely to be anywhere. Last of all
came the horse herd, with three wranglers now — men
especially good with the rifle, for horses were a great
temptation to the raiding war parties.

They were in high country — big country, now.
The scenery was spectacular and growing more so.
Mountains were visible on both the right and the left.
Out of those mountains, the cowboys figured, Indians
might come. They had seen none as yet, but they re-
membered the sage warning of Nelson Story's friend,
Jim Bridger:

"Whar ye don't see no Injuns, thar they're bound to be thickest."

The sagebrush plains with the mountains about them were so elevated — 5000 feet or more above sea level — that the autumn air sometimes grew cold enough to freeze ice on water in a bucket. It was near the first of October, and winter would soon be upon them.

When they came to the Cheyenne River, Story told the men to give the cattle an extra chance to fill themselves with water.

"We've got a long dry drive ahead," he said. "Fill every canteen and keg. I don't know how long it will take us to get to water, but these cattle can walk with any herd that ever came up the trail. The moon is bright these nights, and we'll keep going day and night if we can. Never bed the herd short of midnight. We ought to be able to make twenty-five miles a day with this bunch, and if we can do that it will only be a little more than three days before we have all the water we'll want. They've got to make it, boys."

The men were silent but grim. A long dry drive was always an ordeal, and took the best herd-handling. One thing was in their favor: Story had bought the best kind of riding stock, and they had no fear of their mounts giving out.

But what about the cattle? The first day was not so bad, although the longhorns seemed not to be able to understand why they were driven along at this pace when they should be allowed to graze and rest now and then.

The march was continued by moonlight until Story decided the herd had all it could do for that day. Then the point riders bunched the leading steers, the rest of the cattle came to a halt as they drew up to these, and the longhorns were only too glad to lie down and rest.

But not for long. An hour before dawn they were urged to their feet, and the drive began again. The men had their drinking water rationed, and in getting supper the night before, the cook had used as little as possible, yet already the supply was growing short.

By midday, the cattle were showing signs of suffering. Some of them lolled their tongues despairingly, and an almost continual sullen bawling came from the thirsty beasts. Story was very much worried now, for even if they made another twenty-five miles this day, there were still nearly thirty to go before water could be reached.

Toward the middle of the afternoon one of the point riders came back, his horse galloping in spite of the necessity of saving the mounts as much as possible.

"I rode up on that little butte," he said, pointing. "About ten miles ahead I could see what looks like a creek of some kind. And I can see a little timber scattering along it. There may be water there."

Story took prompt action. He changed mounts and told his point rider to do the same. With these fresher horses they rode out ahead of the bellowing herd.

There was some danger possible in this, for if there was water in that creek, there might also be Indians. But the trail boss had to run the risk.

"No Indians," he said, as they drew near the stream bed. And a little later, "No water, either."

But his companion had ridden down the dry watercourse. He came back presently.

"There's a little water there," he said.

Story felt hopeful as he went with his cowboy. But the hope soon was dispelled by disappointment.

Water there was, a pool of stagnant, scum-covered liquid, the last left perhaps by some rain weeks ago.

"It's not fit for men to drink," he said. "I don't think there's enough even for the horse herd, let alone the cattle."

He thought for a moment.

"You stay here," he said. "I'm going back and I'll send the chuck wagon here. There's a couple of shovels in it, and you and the cook may be able to dig an Indian well in the bottom downstream from this lagoon."

By "Indian well" he meant a hole in the sand through which water, seeping from the befouled pool, would come clean enough from its passage through the sand to be drinkable for men.

"We'll hold the herd," he went on. "When the chuck wagon with all the kegs and canteens has had time to fill up, I'll have the horses brought over. They can at least get a few swallows of water from the pool, and maybe it will carry them through."

Holding the cattle herd was a hard and pathetic task. The longhorns wanted to go, instinctively hoping that somewhere ahead they would find water. They were too dry now to graze. While the chuck wagon went to the creek bed, where an Indian well was quickly and successfully dug, and while the horse herd had its chance to gulp a little of the water, Story watched his cattle suffer.

It seemed forever that the horse watering proceeded, for only a few of the ponies at a time could be allowed at the pool, the others held at a distance to await their turns because the little lagoon was so small that it would have been trampled into undrinkable mud by the larger herd. The night horses of the crew were given especial preference.

Presently the chuck wagon came back, and each of the men was given a canteen of tepid, bad-tasting water with which to quench his thirst. There was some comfort in the thought that the horses would be somewhat refreshed, although every drop of water in the pool had been consumed by them with none having all he wanted.

But now it was time to move on again.

The problem of keeping the herd together became serious. Naturally, the stronger cattle forged ahead and the weaker lagged behind. Story himself rode in the drag now, to save as many laggards as possible, while up ahead the point riders fought to keep the leading steers at a pace slow enough so that the others could keep up.

The dry camp that night was one never to be forgotten. From the herd came a continual noise of distress, and every man in the outfit stayed on horseback throughout the hours of rest, to keep the longhorns together.

Next day, the third without water, the longhorns continued their march. The cattle were a sorry spectacle. Their ribs stood out like basketwork, flanks sagged, tongues hung from mouths, and heads were low. Above the yells and whistles of the cowpunchers rose the bawling, bellowing, and moaning of the thirst-tortured herd.

Here and there losses occurred. An old, weak cow, at the limit of her endurance, would collapse. There was no way to get her up. A mercy shot was the only kindness that could be done for her, and the desert ravens and buzzards soon descended on the carcass as the herd passed on. Again and again weak cattle were thus lost.

To Story it became evident that he could not let the herd even stop for rest this third night. If the cattle ever lay down they would never rise again.

So the suffering drive went on and on. Haggard cowboys, their lips cracked and their eyes bloodshot, kept the longhorns moving. By morning animals and men alike were nearly crazed.

But at dawn they could see that they were at the edge of a wide valley. Only a few miles away thickly growing timber marked the twisting course of a stream.

They were looking at the Powder River!

As the cattle neared water they broke into what was almost a stampede, though their weakness prevented any great speed in their gallop. Up and down the

river they ranged themselves, drinking deeply, thirstily. Some even waded out into the stream as if to cool their fevered feet while they drank.

The dry drive had ended. And the wonderful endurance of the longhorns was shown by the fact that only a few of the weakest of the cattle had been left behind on that terrible march.

CAMP WAS MADE right there, beside the Powder, so
that horses and cattle could fill themselves with fresh
grass, and drink and drink again, to their fill.

To the west could be seen the mighty peaks of the
Big Horn Mountains, and to the east were the columns
of Pumpkin Buttes. Now Nelson Story felt a new
anxiety.

Thus far they had not been troubled by Indians,
chiefly because they had crossed country so dry that
even Indians did not venture into it. But here, in a
well-watered valley, with abundant trees and game,
Indians might be encountered at any time.

They had, in their march, seen much "Indian sign."
The grimmest evidences of the hostile warriors were
the graves of two men beside the trail — men who
had tried to get through to Fort Phil Kearny and were

killed by the Sioux. Other indications of savages were a travois trail — the marks made by horses dragging tepee poles on which, like a crude sled, the Indians carried much of their goods — and a place where a band of Sioux had camped, shown by round barren spots where their lodges had stood and the inmates had tramped down the grass. Both of these last signs were not far from the Powder River valley.

That day a wagon appeared, driven by a French-Canadian who had with him a boy. It was a trapper's wagon, and the man and boy in it had evidently been working the Powder River and its tributaries for fur.

Nelson Story rode over, as the French-Canadian and his boy began unharnessing and preparing to camp some distance from the cowboy camp.

From the French-Canadian, who seemed to be suspicious, he managed to obtain the information that Fort Reno was only about ten miles upstream.

"You'd better come over and camp nearer us," Story said, with a kindly intention, knowing there was acute danger of Indians.

But the trapper refused. "I'm not half as much afraid of Indians as I am of some white men," he said.

It was evident that the rough appearance of Story's crew, after their long drive, did not appeal to him.

There was also the possibility that he had in his wagon something he did not want discovered — such as Indian trade "whiskey." The French-Canadians as a class got on well with the Indians and often married Indian women, and though liquor was forbidden they used it in their trading. The quality of the "whiskey" was invariably bad, but the Indians would trade for it. *

After having had his invitation thus refused, Story returned to his own camp. The cattle, filled with grass and with their thirst fully satisfied, were bedded down. He told his night herders to be doubly watchful.

They were watchful, but that night Indians somehow managed to get close, perhaps up a hidden ravine. All at once a wildly yelping, whooping band of savages whipped their ponies toward the herd, winging arrows at the herders, and waving blankets to stampede the cattle.

---

* To show the awful nature of some of this trade liquor, here is a recipe given by one man for making "Injun whiskey": Take a barrel of water, add three plugs of chewing tobacco, and five bars of soap, stir half a pound of red pepper into the mixture, throw in some dead leaves, and boil it until the liquid turns brown. Then add two gallons of alcohol and two ounces of strychnine, stir it thoroughly, and bottle it. The strychnine, he explained, though a deadly poison, would in this diluted condition give a stimulating effect, which made up for the small quantity of alcohol used. The soap gave it "bead," and the red pepper "bite." The tobacco would produce nausea, which most Indians thought they must feel if they drank the white man's "fire water." Indians would sometimes trade a whole bundle of furs for a bottle of that concoction. It is no wonder that some of them became murderous when crazed by it.

Before the cowboys in camp could get to their horses, the Indians cut out some of the cattle, and drove them up a coulee.

Two herders were down, with arrows in them. Somehow the other herders managed to keep the bulk of the herd from bolting with those the Indians took.

Story's favorite horse, which he called Sancho Panza, was tethered to a wagon wheel. Mounting this horse, which was very fast, he galloped after the Indians, followed by one of the herders.

In less than a mile the two riders sighted the Indians, who of course could travel no faster than the cattle they were herding along. At the same time the Indians sighted them.

At once the warriors deployed in the shape of a crescent, and came back toward the rash white men. Story knew they would surround him and his rider if they stayed where they were, so he began a retreat.

The herder's mount was much slower than Sancho Panza, and was being rapidly overtaken by the mounted Indians. Story later said, "The arrows were going around the herder's head like yellow jackets around a disturbed nest."

To help his cowboy, the trail boss halted behind a large boulder and drew his two revolvers. As the six-shooters began their rapid barking the Indians gave up the pursuit of the herder, and drew off. The man was not wounded, but he would have been killed had not Story defended him against his pursuers.

Nelson Story was a born fighter. As Catlin later said of him, "Even after three years on the skirmish line in the Civil War, I have never seen a fighting man like Nelson Story. He was always splendidly mounted and would ride like the wind. He would say, 'Come on, boys,' and we'd follow. But accustomed as the Civil War had made me to follow almost any dare-devil leader, there were a good many times when Nelson Story had me guessing."

This was one of those times. Story posted a few men

to hold the herd, and with every other rider in his outfit pursued those Indians and his cattle.

The trail of the running longhorns was easy to
follow. It led toward the Bad Lands. As it later turned
out the raiders were a rather small hunting party from
a large camp near the Pumpkin Buttes. Evidently they
did not dream they would be followed.

The vengeful cowboys came upon them "grouped
around a campfire, eating from one of the cattle which
they had killed and partially roasted."

It was a complete surprise. In every direction the
Indians bolted, but the Remingtons made deadly
havoc among them.

Nelson Story and his men returned to their camp
on the Powder River, driving the missing cattle before
them.

Years after, John Catlin told of this counter-raid.

"How many cattle did you lose?" he was asked.

"Not a single head," he answered. "We just followed
those Indians into the Bad Lands and got the cattle
back."*

---

* In one respect Catlin's memory was faulty. Not all the cattle were
recovered. There was the steer the Indians had butchered to eat. One
or two cattle, wounded by Indian arrows, had to be slaughtered, fur-
nishing food for the outfit in the next days.

"Did they yield them willingly?" was the next question.

"Well, you might say so," Catlin grinned. "We surprised them in their camp, and they weren't in shape to protest much against our taking the cattle."

Both Catlin and Story were under the impression that they accounted for all of the raiders. It is true that most of the Indians were too dead to argue, but some must have escaped. If so they did not stop running until they reached the main camp at Pumpkin Buttes.

The reason for this statement is that the results of the affair became known to the Sioux and Cheyennes, along with the story of the guns that would fire so fast that "a man could hardly count the number of bullets" which they sent with deadly effect; also that the white men with that particular cattle herd shot hard and true. This information could hardly have been transmitted by dead men. Perhaps the reputation thus built by the reports of the survivors was of great help to Story's outfit in the days that followed.

After they returned from punishing the raiders, Story and some of his men rode to the camp of the French-Canadian and his boy. Both were dead, scalped and mutilated. All their goods of any value to the Indians were gone, including their horses, and the wagon was burned.

The bodies were buried by Story's men, and the boss sent a messenger to Fort Reno, to get an ambulance for his two men. Two had died — the French-Canadian and his boy — and two had been wounded in that brief raid. The injured cowboys were left in the post hospital at Fort Reno, and both eventually recovered, though neither went on to Montana.

Next day the march was resumed, the long caravan of cattle, riders, and wagons in motion after crossing the shallow river, the water of which was reddish with clay, cottonwoods growing thickly on its banks.

Presently the cowboys could see Fort Reno. They must have been surprised at the run-down condition of this so-called military post. The fort was originally built by General Connor in his unsuccessful campaign of the year before, and in spite of some improvements by Colonel Carrington, was in a state of disrepair. Its buildings were of crooked cottonwood logs chinked with mud, and all were mud-roofed. There was a high stake fence — not really a parapet and more to keep livestock in than to keep Indians out.

At first the garrison was composed of "Galvanized

Yanks" — a term given to Confederate soldiers captured during the Civil War, who, rather than go to prison, volunteered to fight, so long as they did not have to fight against the South. These men were assigned to duty on the hostile Indian frontier. They were good fighters and good soldiers, but with the war over they wanted to go home.

This wish was granted by the government. They received their discharges when Carrington arrived with his expedition, and marched back to civilization. Carrington garrisoned the post with two companies of his own soldiers, and placed Captain Joshua Proctor in command.

Proctor was elderly, gray-bearded, and worried — as he had good reason to be. The Indians had not neglected his post. Frequently they had raided and bushwhacked around Fort Reno. Just a little while before Story's arrival they had run off a herd of horses and mules. Troops pursuing them could not overtake them and returned empty-handed.

"It's the height of foolishness to venture farther into this hostile country," he told Story.

The trail boss thanked him for his advice, then told his men to start the herd. The next fort would be Phil Kearny.

Evidences of the hostility of the Indians increased. At a creek with the strange name of Crazy Woman were the graves of two soldiers slain the previous July. A little farther along at Clear Creek was found another grave — that of a wagon master named Dillon, who was with the last wagon train to pass along the Bozeman Trail before it was closed by the Sioux. Dillon was killed by Indians.

Signal smokes were seen frequently in the surrounding hills, and the men knew they were being watched by painted enemies. But for some reason they were not attacked before they reached Fort Phil Kearny, then just being completed.

This fort was large and quite elaborate for the time and country. Built of logs, its heavy stockade had blockhouses at each corner, and within those walls were no less than thirty buildings, including barracks, a chapel, guardhouse, hospital, officers' quarters, and cavalry stables.

Carrington planned it elaborately, but the place he chose was six miles from the nearest pine timber, and all those logs had to be felled and then hauled to the fort, under dangerous conditions, for the Indians made frequent attacks on the wood train and its escort, and lives were lost as a result.

Now, as the herd came in sight of the fort, Story saw a column of horsemen in blue issue from the main gate. They were soldiers, and they rode at a cavalry trot directly for his outfit.

He did not know what their errand was, but he felt concern. A vague feeling that there might be trouble ahead for him filled him as he spurred his horse forward to meet the troopers.

The officer in the lead threw up a gauntleted hand to command a halt, and as Story rode up he found himself facing the commander of all the troops along the Bozeman Trail, including not only those at Fort Phil Kearny, but those at Fort Reno to the south, and Fort C. F. Smith to the north, Colonel Carrington himself.

Colonel Henry B. Carrington was a small man, which is nothing against him — many great soldiers have been short, including Napoleon Bonaparte and Ulysses S. Grant. Unfortunately Carrington was not, and probably never could become, a great soldier. He was thin-faced, with a long dark beard, and beneath his high forehead his eyes bulged slightly, giving him a look of being startled or afraid.

As a matter of fact, he was afraid. Carrington was not a combat officer. He was a political soldier, and though he held a brevet major general's rank in the Civil War, he had never seen a battle. All his time was spent in the North, recruiting regiments, setting up prisoner-of-war camps, and prosecuting Copperheads — a name given, in the Union States, to Southern sympathizers.

After the war was over, late in 1865, Carrington, by pulling wires with influential political friends in Washington, was given top rank in this western expedition, over the heads of many battle-tested officers who were not only more deserving, but better qualified than he.

Now that he was in command, he probably wished he was not. He was following orders and building forts, but he was fussy and indecisive, and the way Sioux war parties kept prowling around his post made him even more nervous. So active and daring had been the Indians that although Carrington brought more than two hundred horses to Fort Phil Kearny, only forty were left by October 10, when Story and his outfit arrived. Of seven hundred cattle brought, six hundred had been swept away by the red raiders. And on that day his adjutant reported there were only fourteen rounds of ammunition per man at the post.

Small wonder that Carrington was worried, even though he knew that relief was on the way and more ammunition and provisions would soon reach him. As a matter of fact, the worst was still to come in the future, for the following December Captain Fetterman's detachment would be annihilated so close to the fort that the roar of the guns in the battle would be clearly heard there.

But now, for some reason, the Colonel seemed rather to take out his irritation on Nelson Story.

"Proceed no farther," he ordered.

"When can I go on?" asked the young trail boss.

"When you receive my permission," said the Colonel shortly.

"How soon will that be?"

"My orders," said Carrington, "are that no party shall go on from this post unless it contains at least forty men."

"You mean I've got to wait here until another train comes along?" demanded Story indignantly. "This late in the season there may not be another one!"

(As a matter of fact no other train went up that trail in 1866, or for two or three years afterward.)

"You are only twenty-nine men strong," said Carrington.

"But look here —" Story protested. "We're all armed with these new Remington breech-loaders. That gives us firepower equal to a hundred men with your army Springfields."

"You will obey my orders!" snapped Carrington.

As the young man stared at him, he added, "You will corral your stock three miles from the fort until you get further instructions."

"Three miles from the stockade?" gasped the astounded Story. "For what reason?"

"Because the post's animals need the grass near the fort," said Carrington coldly, and rode away with his men.

Nelson Story stared after him. Where he had expected friendship and perhaps help, he had suddenly encountered an obstruction that seemed worse to him than flooded rivers, stampedes, Jayhawkers, dry drives, and hostile Indians.

Almost with despair he thought of his situation. If he held his cattle and horses three miles from the fort, as Carrington commanded, he and his men were too far away to expect help from the soldiers in case Indians attacked. Furthermore, it was now the middle of October. The Big Horn Mountains already were white with snow down almost to their bases, the first frosts had nipped all the trees in the valleys, turning cottonwood and aspen leaves yellow, and a blizzard might come roaring down in a white smother of snow, wind-blown and arctic-cold, where he and his outfit were being told to camp. His men were thinly clad in their Texas clothes, and so was he, while cattle invariably drifted before severe snowstorms.

Nevertheless, he decided to obey the Colonel's orders, since he hardly knew what else to do. So he set his men to work cutting poplar and cottonwood

poles to make two corrals — a large one for the longhorns, and a smaller one for the horses and work oxen.
In the daytime the animals could be herded outside
to graze, always keenly watched by men alert for any
signs of Indians. At night they were penned inside
the fences.

The corral could not have been much, hastily built
as it was, and could easily have been broken down.
But it shortly proved its value.

In the darkness of a frosty night, while Story's men
stayed close to the chuck wagon fire and their own
little campfires, a darker shadow seemed to gather

among the shadows of the nearer woods. Had the two men who rode as sentinels around the corrals noticed it, they might have thought it a herd of elk, or even buffalo.

It was, in reality, a stealthy band of Sioux, advancing slowly and cautiously toward the corrals, their horses at a walk, their weapons ready. Suddenly there was a warning shout from one of the sentinels.

Instantly the slowly moving shadow broke into separate parts as the Indians, knowing themselves discovered, scattered with their yelping war cries, and charged.

Flashes of fire spurted from the oncoming array, and the reports of guns echoed from the mountains.

Story's men leaped for their rifles, but already the Indians were at the corrals. The horse herd was their objective, and for a time they could not be reached successfully by bullets from the cowpunchers because they were screened by the ponies which circled, galloping, inside their corral.

In that brief period one of the two sentinels went down. Then the Indians, finding the horses were corralled, galloped away as rapidly as they came. Too late the fire of the Remingtons could be brought to bear. In the darkness, and with such rapidly moving targets, not an Indian was hit.

But Story and his men found one of the two sentinel riders — the one who gave the alarm — dead beside the horse corral, scalped and pin-cushioned with arrows.

The corrals had saved the outfit from a general stampede, although if the engagement had lasted much longer some panic-stricken steer might have lunged with his full weight against the frail barrier and broken it down, releasing the whole herd.

One of Story's men said later, "There were three hundred troops at the fort. But the Indians were more afraid of us than they were of the soldiers. We were armed with Remington breech-loaders, and the troops had only Springfield rifles. The little brush we had with the Indians near Fort Reno taught them something of the effectiveness of our fire and got them scared."

There was no such overconfidence in Nelson Story's mind, and the death of the cowboy, whom they buried next day, caused him to reach a big decision.

He was sure now that if he remained at this place much longer, a more powerful force of Sioux would come and destroy him and his men. What should he do? Stay where he was? Already he had decided against that. Return the way he came? He could not. By hardest work and through many dangers he had brought his longhorns more than twelve hundred miles, and he was too close to his goal to give up now.

The military officers had warned him that there were not fewer than three thousand bloody-minded warriors blocking the trail up ahead, and that the soldiers, though armed "with the best Springfield rifle-muskets," did not dare venture from the fort — a danger which was not exaggerated, as events proved.

But danger or no danger, Nelson Story *had* to go on. The fate of his men and of all his hopes and plans rested squarely on his shoulders.

On the night of October 22 he called his men together, and laid the situation before them.

"I'm going to ask for a vote," he said. "Shall we continue to abide by Carrington's orders or move out in spite of them, and take our chances by heading for Montana? All in favor of starting out tonight say 'Aye.' Opposed, 'No.'"

Every single man in the outfit shouted "Aye," except one. His name was George Dow, and he said "No."

The word was hardly out of his mouth when he found himself looking into the muzzle of Story's six-shooter.

"Tie him up," the trail boss ordered. "Now put him on his horse."

His men obeyed.

"Now let's get moving," said Story.

At once the cattle and spare horses swung out of the corrals, and the wagons followed them, as they pointed northeast along the Bozeman Trail toward Fort C. F. Smith, seventy-five miles away.

All that night they drove, making a wide circle around the fort before striking the trail on the other side. Story did not intend that Carrington should see him and perhaps send troops after him to put him under arrest for disobeying orders.

During this march George Dow rode with his hands bound behind him and a good man leading his horse and keeping an eye on him. By morning they were fifteen miles along the trail, so far from Fort Phil Kearny that Story believed the danger of being followed was past. He cantered his mount back to the disconsolate prisoner.

"Untie him," he said.

Dow's bonds were removed.

"Now, George," said Story, "you're free to ride back to the fort, if you want to."

But Dow had been thinking. Perhaps he was a little ashamed; and besides, that ride back alone might be dangerous.

"I reckon I'll stay with you, boss," he said.

So the outfit stayed together, and George Dow was admitted again into full companionship.*

At Fort Phil Kearny, the morning of October 23, Carrington learned to his surprise and anger that Nelson Story, with his herd and his outfit, had stolen out in the night and gone on against orders. The Colonel first commanded that a detachment of soldiers should ride after the trail drivers and bring them back. But when he considered how shorthanded he was at the fort, he countermanded the order and Story was not pursued.

---

* Story never again mentioned to Dow his disloyalty. On the contrary, in later years when Dow was old and poor, he received a check for five dollars each month signed by Nelson Story.

8

NELSON STORY had taken a trail which he knew would be the most dangerous he had yet traversed. It would lead them across the Tongue River and the Little Big Horn River. At the Tongue they would pass near the place where, the previous year, a detachment of soldiers had been surprised by a Sioux war party and Captain O. F. Cole killed. The Little Big Horn was to be famous for the defeat given General George Armstrong Custer, in which every member of his immediate command was wiped out on June 25, 1876.

Of more imminent peril was the fact that in the headwaters of those streams, where they flowed out from the mountains, were the great winter encampments of the Indians. Story ordered that the cattle be allowed to graze during the day, and trailed only at night. The grazing and resting place was always

some valley, while watchers on the rim about it kept
a nervous and sharp eye out for hostile Indians.

The men all knew they were practically in the reach
of a huge horde of Sioux and Cheyenne; and the
slightest accident might bring an overwhelming force
of the savages down on them. There was no way, of
course, to still the cattle, who bawled and lowed as
usual, completely unconscious of the overhanging
peril.

Yet by an almost incredible piece of good luck —
although they did not know it at the time — the whole
outfit of men, wagons, cattle, and horses passed within
a few miles of where Red Cloud's main hostile camp
was pitched, without being seen by an Indian.

The occasion for this good fortune was that winter,
which sets in early in the mountain country, descended
just at this time with its first cold snap. There was
no snow, but icy winds blew.

The Indians, in that first cold weather, felt inclined
to keep to the comfort of their tepees. Added to this
was another fortunate occurrence. Additional Sioux
and Cheyennes had just come from the north, and the
warriors and women already encamped in their warm
lodges were greeting these newcomers with primitive
hospitality.

These facts are known from the later accounts of the Indians themselves. There had been a good fall hunt, and plenty of winter meat was in. The friends from the north were welcomed joyfully, there was much visiting between tepee and tepee, and between the villages, with feasting on roast buffalo, some little gambling by means of simple Indian games,* and perhaps some of the youths and maidens seized the chance for a little flirting.

Meantime the newly arrived chiefs from the north were sitting in council tepees with chiefs already on the ground, including Red Cloud himself, planning stratagems against the white men — stratagems one of which would lure Fetterman's command into a trap from which none returned.

The feasting was so pleasant, the weather so unpleasant, that the young men stayed in camp for those few days. The young warriors always were the reckless outriders, looking for adventure, and had it not been for that late October cold snap these "wolves," as

* To show the simplicity of these games, one of the favorites in the plains tribes was called "Hand." It was played exactly as small children play by hiding a button or penny in one hand and holding both out for the other to guess which contains it. If the guess is right, the holder loses; if wrong, he wins. Cheyennes and Sioux played this game with a small piece of bone, worn smooth by use. On such guesses were wagered high stakes for a poor people — blankets, robes, lodges, guns, ponies, even wives.

the Indians called their scouts, could not have failed to see the long, dusty procession of cattle, wagons, and riders on the Bozeman Trail.

The end of the cold snap came just before the last of the month. On October 31, Colonel Carrington, at Fort Phil Kearny ordered a celebration of the completion of the fort. On that day one chronicler wrote: "October 31 was ideal for a celebration day, the sun rising out of a clean azure sky, turning the air soft and balmy and brightening the golden leaves of aspens on the Big Horn slopes."

There was a review of the troops, a flag raising, a band concert, a speech by the commanding officer, and a salute by cannon at the fort. This brought some Indians out to see what the shooting was about. They were observed galloping their ponies around the base of the Sullivant Hills, to the west, and men stood to arms. But the Indians returned to their camps without any skirmishing, their curiosity satisfied.

By that day Nelson Story's longhorn herd had passed the point of greatest danger, and was well on its way through the pass between the Big Horn Mountains and the Wolf Mountains, toward Fort C. F. Smith.

As the outfit traveled along it continued to see evidence of the fierce purpose of the Indians. On the

Tongue River was the grave of a victim of the hostile warriors, and not long before reaching Fort C. F. Smith the men found the graves of five more who had been killed by the savages, partly dug up and eaten by wolves. Near the Big Horn River was the grave of a wagon driver, and on a creek running into the Yellowstone four graves were marked with headboards giving the names of those buried there:

Reverend W. K. Thomas, age 36 years, of Belleville, Ill. Chas. K. Thomas, age 8 years, of Belleville, Ill. James Schultz, age 35 years, of Ottawa (Canada.) C. K. Wright — All killed and scalped by Indians on the 24th day of August, 1865.

These were by no means all the graves, nor did they include the many graves in the post cemeteries at Fort Phil Kearny and Fort C. F. Smith. That list of deaths was a grim one, but the cowboys rode on with their herd, watchful and ready to fight if necessary.

When they reached the Big Horn River, on the banks of which stood Fort C. F. Smith, Nelson Story estimated he had come thirteen hundred miles or more, and that only about two hundred and fifty miles remained to Virginia City. At this fort no effort was made by the soldiers to stop them. In fact the ferry was put into use to transport the wagons across the stream.

The Big Horn at this point and during this season was not a large stream. The water was icy, but the cowboys yipped and urged the cattle into it, and the herd splashed over, hardly needing to swim although the saddle skirts of the riders were wet by the time they got across.

Once across the Big Horn and a day or so along their way, the men felt that they were past the greatest danger and almost to their goal. There was a spirit of jubilance among them.

Only Nelson Story looked anxious. He was surveying a gray cloud bank toward the west which appeared to be overspreading the sky.

"It might be bad," he said to himself.

Better than anyone in his outfit he knew what the full fury of a mountain blizzard was.

Something caused a panic of cattle up front, and the cowboys rode hard to stop the possible stampede. Two or three buffalo bulls were on the trail, looking huge and dangerous, with their great humps, thick woolly manes, and sharp curved horns. Cattle could not stand the sight of them, but a half a dozen of Story's cowboys rode at them, waving lariats and firing six-shooters in the air.

They had no desire to kill the animals, particularly on this trail, for cattle grow crazy at the smell of blood. The blood-bellow of a herd is one of the most fearsome sounds in nature. Some savage instinct seems to possess the beasts. A single blood-soaked cowhide has been known to bring longhorns into a milling, bawling, unmanageable mass, all giving vent to a combination of scream and bellow, and so excited that the greatest difficulty was met in getting them to move on.

As for the buffalo, they looked stupidly at the on-coming cowboys. Then, as if realizing for the first time that danger might be approaching, they swung awkwardly around and galloped at surprising speed, considering their bulk, in the direction from which they came.

The cowboys wanted them completely off that trail. It was a hot race before the buffalo could be headed up into the mountains where they were pursued long enough so there would be no danger of their return before the herd passed.

All this took time, and by the time the outfit was on the move again — the lead steers still snorting and nervous — the sky was completely overcast. Little flecks of white began coming down.

"Snow!" exclaimed a Texan, who had never seen snow before but had heard of it.

"Going to get colder?" asked another.

"It might," said Story.

The snow grew thicker, driving from the west, in which direction the cattle were heading. At first it did not seem to bother them a great deal, although their backs soon grew white.

But there was a wind behind it, keen as a knife. The cowboys took turns putting on all the warm clothes they had — tying bandannas around their heads under their hats to protect their ears, slipping on any spare clothes they possessed, and donning their yellow slickers, which they tied about their waists with hobble ropes. Even so, they were poorly clad for weather if it grew very cold.

And cold it grew. The snowflakes became a whirling fog of white, thickening to a powder of razor-sharp crystals, a choking smother, swept along by a hurricane wind. Down went the thermometer until it registered below zero.

The cattle? They had been bred for no such climate as this. As the knife-edge gale swept level across the land with its choking burden of snow, they began to do what Story had dreaded. One after another they began to turn, their rumps toward the storm, drifting with it. Nothing the men could do would make them face it.

Cattle will always drift with a storm, while buffalo will always head into it, since their heavy wool is on the forward parts of their bodies and their heads. To drift was the only chance for the cattle, and the cowboys could only hope to keep the herd together, and prevent it from drifting too fast.

Snowdrifts began to build up in the coulees, and

through these, headed by Nelson Story, the riders plunged, swearing, whooping, sometimes laughing, keeping up with the bellowing, huddling herd which moved stubbornly along the trail up which it had come.

All that night the terrifying migration continued. Story knew that if it did not cease his cattle might go over some cliff, pushed by those behind, or perish in a river, or at the very least become so scattered they could not be gathered again.

There was no sleep in this crisis for anyone. With

numbing hands and legs the cowboys rode and rode. The chuck wagon turned and followed, and when he could, the cook made hot coffee to warm the men.

Through those long night hours Story feared his whole great effort would end in ruin. But toward morning, glancing toward the west with eyes reddened from the icy wind, he thought the sky was lightening a little. Could he hope for so much? Sometimes blizzards might last for days, even a week, and if this one did, nothing would survive it.

In an hour or so there was no question. The clouds were breaking up, and gradually the snow grew less, then ceased, while the wind died down to at least a moderate rate. Luck had smiled on the outfit once more. Gradually the half-frozen cowboys halted the cattle. Eventually the herd was turned and began, unwilling and cold, to retrace the steps over which it had drifted during the storm.

Nelson Story was profoundly thankful for the break in the weather. That storm, which swept all the way down across Wyoming, was serious enough so that a few days later Colonel Carrington, at Fort Phil Kearny, wrote a complaining message to Fort Laramie:

"My mail [from Fort Laramie] was twelve days [on the road], on account of snow, bad roads, and weather . . . It must not be overlooked that our snows, which leave the hills bare [blown off by the winds] fill the . . . ravines, valleys and gulches, so that no one can travel. There are snowdrifts four feet deep in ravines within a mile of the fort."

But Nelson Story, who with his men faced that same storm under the worst conditions possible, made no complaint. He was too glad that he had come out of it without a great disaster.

Another peril threatened very soon.

The cattle made their way slowly on toward the Yellowstone Crossing, taking time to graze where the wind had left the ground bare of snow. The weather moderated. Then, without warning, a wild array of riders appeared from the piney woods — thin, wiry horses, swarthy horsemen with round shields, gleaming weapons, and fluttering headdresses.

One of the herders, seeing the Indians, fired his six-shooter as a warning. At that a shrill chorus of whoops came from the savages, as they rode forward.

But Story and his men were ready for them. Leaving just enough to guard the cattle, the others galloped out between the herd and the Indians.

A few gunshots came from the hostile band, without

damage, for the range was too great for old-fashioned muskets.

Then the Remington rifles took a hand. The cowboys knew their weapons, and in the sudden fusillade of rapid fire the Indians were stunned and cowed. The Remingtons far outranged the few Indian muskets, and confusion was seen in the ranks of the savages as warriors were hit here and there.

In a few minutes it was over. Away fled the Indians, carrying with them such of their friends as had been hit. That particular band never again molested Story's outfit.

Not a man nor an animal was lost by Story, as the march began again, and the cowboys were gleeful over having taught the Indians such a lesson that they did not expect they would ever come back.

The trail drivers were mistaken. One more tragedy still awaited the weary and weather-beaten outfit.

The herd was marching by day now, finding grass in the valleys, though the mountains were white with snow and the nights very cold. Some time after the brush with the large Indian band, a crossing was made at Clark's Fork, really simple because it was only a relatively shallow ford. The outfit drove on, and then, one crisp, bright morning, a shot was heard far ahead.

One of the men had ridden forward, hoping to get a deer for the camp mess. This might be his shot at a buck.

But something told Nelson Story differently. Spurring his horse he galloped hard for a rise just ahead. Suddenly he heard the shrill hooting yelps that told him of Indians.

He topped the rise just in time to see a sight that filled him with anger and horror. On the ground lay the hunter, shot off his horse. A band of fifteen or twenty Indians was riding toward him at a dead run.

Too far away to help even with a rifle, Story saw the savages swoop down on the prostrate man. Two of them rode up, one on each side of the hunter, reached down, and taking him under the arms, galloped off with him, the others following with yells of triumph.

Story whirled his horse and waved an arm toward his men. Several rode hard to join him. Together they raced to the rescue, hoping against hope that they might still save their comrade.

They were too late. The Indians were gone. Behind them on a little hill, dead and scalped, lay their victim. His body was nailed to the ground by an arrow through his chest.

Nothing could be done. The men cursed furiously

and helplessly, buried their friend, and the herd went on.

This was the fourth trail driver lost — the two wounded and left at Fort Reno, the one killed near Fort Phil Kearny, and now this man. It was bitter medicine, yet everyone in that outfit realized how very lucky they had been. Courage, boldness, constant vigilance, and above all, good fortune, had been with them, or all of them might be dead somewhere back along that trail.

Soon after this tragedy the herd forded and swam the Yellowstone River, then at low ebb, near the mouth

of the Stillwater River, where Columbus, Montana , now stands.

A day or so later, about December 1, a magnificent wide valley opened before them. To the north stood the jagged upthrust of the Crazy Mountains; west loomed the craggy Big Belt Range; and south the towering Absaroka Mountains thrust their peaks upward.

Sheltered by these gigantic natural windbreaks, with the crystal-clear Shields River running through it to the Yellowstone, wood and water plentiful, and rich grass for cattle to fatten on, it was a cattleman's dream of a range.

"There boys!" said Story. "There's where we'll build our ranch!"

He had chosen the place long before, and he appointed young Tom Thompson foreman, and set a crew to building log cabins for ranch headquarters. The longhorns scattered gratefully to enjoy their ease and graze their fill.

All except a small herd of prime steers — for Nelson Story had not reached the end of his trail. He had a very important errand to do.

Ellen Story had been lonely at Virginia City. In

the months since she kissed her husband goodbye and saw him go off southward with his box of gold, she had no idea where he was, or what he was doing, or indeed if he was still alive. But she kept busy and managed to appear cheerful, like the fine girl she was, although the long suspense and worry made her heart ache.

As for Virginia City itself, the town was cut off more than ever from civilization by the Indian war. Men were much concerned, and rumors were always in the air, even while they continued to work their rich gold placers. There was talk about smoke signals seen on distant buttes, and sometimes men who were too bold in their prospecting trips failed to return.

It is not to be wondered that when, on December 9, gunshots and yells were heard, every man leaped for his nearest weapon.

Ellen Story went to the door of her cabin. She could hear questions being asked.

"What is it?"

"An Indian attack?"

"Are the outlaws back again?"

Terrified women clutched their babies to their breasts and called their older children to get indoors.

Then there was a sudden pounding of hoofs, and galloping down the street came cattle — wide-horned, wild-eyed, snorting and bellowing. Behind them rode horsemen, emptying their revolvers in the air and whooping with joy. Last of all rumbled wagons, carrying food and goods.

Incredulous jubilation replaced terror. Those were longhorn steers, brought all the way from Texas, and the riders were cowboys, grinning and delighted at reaching this destination!

But Ellen had eyes for only one of those wild horse-men. She saw Nelson Story ride straight toward her. Before the door of her house he brought his horse to its haunches in a sliding stop. Then he leaped from the saddle and ran, bounding, toward her. In a moment she was caught up in his arms.

All the rest of that day and night Virginia City celebrated the incredible event. Mining towns always went wild on great occasions, and this one was especially great.

Music was called for. From the saloons and dance halls fiddlers appeared in the streets, and with them a few battered horns and a drum so that there was an orchestra of sorts, which made up for its lack of musical polish with its enthusiasm.

Dance hall girls, scantily clad though they were, danced in the street with bounding placer diggers. Wives of bearded miners forgot to be staid and proper, and danced also. Where men could not find women, they danced with each other, one of each pair having a handkerchief tied around his arm to signify that he was the "woman" of that couple.

Up and down the length of the street, Story's riders were the heroes of the day. Nothing was too good for them, and as for the Texans, they had ridden long and far, and now they diverted themselves. Drinks were free, and they could not spend their money, even though their boss had recently given them their full wages.

They danced with the dance hall girls, they danced with the proper housewives, they danced with miners, they even danced with each other. All up and down that long, crooked street they cavorted, adding their whoops to the roars of the miners. And next morning some of them nursed headaches most severe.

Nelson Story did not dance. He came to the door once or twice, his arm around Ellen's waist, with a grin splitting his face, to acknowledge cheers which rose in a storm of approval.

But he preferred for that night the company of his wife, and they sat and talked long of all that had happened, happy to be together, while Virginia City raved outside. The greatest cattle drive of all time was over. Well did Nelson Story merit rest and the joy of being home again.

WHAT WAS the later fate of Nelson Story and those who were with him in his adventures?

As to Nelson and Ellen Story, they did not long remain in Virginia City. The beef steers and merchandise he took there were quickly sold; and the couple went to the little town then called Missouri, which Story renamed Bozeman, after his friend John Bozeman, when the latter was killed by Indians a year later.

At first the couple lived with a Methodist minister, the Reverend Mr. Byrd, and his wife, in a small cabin about a mile and a half from Bozeman. But the Indians grew so troublesome that they had to move into the town.

Story befriended Mr. Byrd and helped him get established. Some years later the minister saved Story's life when a man named Huntsman, who had been discharged for dishonesty, tried to murder him. Mr. Byrd pushed the would-be killer's rifle aside just as the trigger was pulled. Though the bullet ripped a hole in Story's jacket it did not wound him, and he thereupon gave Huntsman a thorough thrashing with his bare fists.

The store at Bozeman was profitable, and with that as a nucleus Story laid out the present city. At one time he traveled over Montana, seeking to have Bozeman made the state capital, but Helena was chosen instead.

At first Story divided his time between his store and home, and the Ox Yoke ranch, the headquarters of which, a cluster of log buildings and corrals, was built near present-day Livingston, Montana. But other affairs caused him to devote himself more and more to his ranch and business. From the original drove of cattle brought from Texas, roughly 1000 head (including calves), the herd grew to 18,000 animals bearing the Ox Yoke brand, grazing up and down the Yellowstone Valley as far as the Crow reservations near Billings, Montana.

John Catlin and Steve Grover, the Indiana ex-soldiers who helped drive cattle and fight Indians with

Story, went on west from Virginia City. Grover continued his journey to Spokane, Washington, where he settled.

Catlin, however, stayed in Idaho until later in life when he moved to Missoula, Montana. He commanded the citizen volunteers in the Battle of Big Hole, when troops under General John Gibbon fought Chief Joseph and his Nez Percé Indians, August 9, 1877. It was perhaps at that time that he received his title of "Major," but he commented wryly of that engagement, "I want to say that we were beautifully whipped."

The young Canadian, Tom Thompson, remained as foreman of the Ox Yoke outfit until 1879, when, while bravely trying to rescue a cowhand named Gage who got into difficulties as they were swimming a herd across the Yellowstone, he met death himself by drowning, a fate all too common in those times. He was buried in the Story family cemetery plot at Bozeman.

George Dow, who went along on the march from Fort Phil Kearny after looking into the muzzle of Story's revolver, remained around Bozeman, a sort of hanger-on of his "boss," whom he came to admire very much.

Of others who made that famous drive not much is known. Many of the Texans remained as permanent residents of Montana, and some of them continued to work for Story. That he took care of them well can be guessed from the way he treated men like Carter and Dow who had hardly been loyal to him.

The drive itself made records in many ways. After Nelson Story reached the end of his long and perilous journey, the Bozeman Trail closed up behind him as if a door had been slammed shut, with hostile Indians watching in deadly readiness to kill any who traveled it. Not for four more years would another trail herd pass up the Powder River valley.

Nevertheless, Story had shown the way. He was accorded the honor of starting the range cattle industry in Montana, and John Walk, another prominent cattleman, later stated that Story was the largest cattle owner in the country until he disposed of his stock and brand after the severe winters of 1886–87.

As soon as the Indian troubles abated, others followed Story's example. The results were momentous. In the next twenty years the hoofs of hundreds of thousands of longhorns cut deep trails all over the West.

They hammered out not only the Sedalia Trail, but

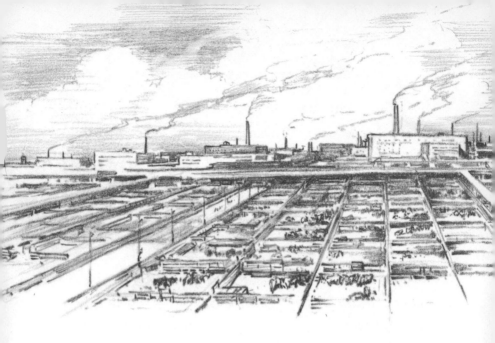

the Chisholm and Dodge City Trails to railhead markets. They beat deep and wide the Western Trail which took herds to Wyoming and Montana; the Goodnight-Loving Trail into Colorado; the Horsehead Route to the Pecos country; the New Mexico–Arizona Trail; and the long, long California Trail. Great packing plants sprang up to process the meat of those cattle, and American families found they could once more afford to buy beef for their tables.

Notable cow-towns sprang up along those cattle trails — towns like Abilene, Ellsworth, Wichita, Fort Hays, and Dodge City, all in Kansas; Ogallala in Nebraska; Cheyenne and Buffalo in Wyoming; Miles City and Billings in Montana; El Paso, Amarillo, and Fort Worth in Texas; as well as many more. Each had its brief period of vivid history, for cowboys were turbulent and so were frontier settlers.

Those were the days when legends were born concerning marshals like Bear River Tom Smith, Wyatt Earp, Wild Bill Hickok, Bat Masterson, Bill Tilghman, and Pat Garrett, among others; and their opposite numbers, gun fighters like John Wesley Hardin, Ben Thompson, Rowdy Joe Lowe, Breed Kenedy, King Fisher, Johnny Ringo, Bill Longley, and Billy the Kid (concerning whom the television versions of today go about as far from the truth as it is possible to get).

Far more important than the gun fighting and excitement of the six-shooter era was the fact that the spread of the cattle industry over the entire West brought about, at least indirectly, the subjugation of hostile Indian tribes, and opened the great plains and mountains to farmers, ranchmen, industries, towns and cities.

It is not too much to say that the longhorns and their trail drivers had a greater and more lasting effect on history than did even the gold rushes.

Nelson Story, who took part in both the gold rushes and the cattle drives, lived to become famous, and died a millionaire. He and Ellen lived at Bozeman, where they reared a fine family and had many devoted friends. Members of the Story family are today among the most respected and prosperous citizens of Montana.

When at last Story retired from the cattle business, he invested wisely in real estate, some of it in the fast-growing city of Los Angeles, California, and from that he prospered enormously. He cared nothing for politics or he might have been governor or senator in Montana.

Instead, he lived out his life, honored by all, "the last of the cattle kings." Both he and Ellen lived to a fine old age. Ellen died in 1924, and Nelson Story, his work done, followed her to the beyond in 1926. Their life together had been filled with adventure, and they left a mark such as few have left on the great West.

Some Books To Read

YOUNG readers interested in the great era of the cattle drives have a large choice of books to read, in their public or school libraries. Some that the author suggests are:

Burt, Struthers, POWDER RIVER.
Cook, James, FIFTY YEARS ON THE OLD FRONTIER.
Dobie, J. Frank, A VAQUERO OF THE BRUSH COUNTRY.
Dobie, J. Frank, THE LONGHORNS.
Hunter, J. Martin, THE TRAIL DRIVERS OF TEXAS.
McCoy, Joseph G., HISTORIC SKETCHES OF THE CATTLE TRADE.
Rollins, Philip Ashton, THE COWBOY.
Wellman, Paul I., THE TRAMPLING HERD.

INDEX